John Ashworth,

   With thanks for talking
about 'Chapman and Hall today'
at an Anniversary Reception, (150 years),
Stationers Hall, London.

   Richard Stileman.

                      June 4th 1980

Cell Differentiation

J.M. Ashworth

Professor of Biology
University of Essex

Chapman and Hall
London

First published in 1973
by Chapman and Hall Ltd
11 New Fetter Lane, London EC4P 4EE
© *1973 J.M. Ashworth*
Reprinted 1975
Printed in Great Britain by
William Clowes & Sons Limited
London, Colchester and Beccles

ISBN 0 412 11760 6

Distributed in the U.S.A.
by Halsted Press, a Division
of John Wiley & Sons, Inc.
New York

Contents

1 Introduction

The development of an embryo is one of the most awe inspiring biological phenomena and the study of cell differentiation can be traced back in antiquity to Aristotle and beyond. However, there are few modern sciences which pay more than a cursory obeisance to their founders and few students seem very interested in the theories of their dead predecessors. Embryology, though, is that rare exception – a science where the problems, theories and often techniques that excite our interest today, are essentially the same as those which excited our colleagues of fifty or even a hundred years ago. They defined the problems and gave them the names that we use today and a brief summary of the way in which a 'typical' animal egg develops will serve to introduce and put in perspective our modern ideas of how cell differentiation occurs.

The frog's egg, like other eggs, is a highly specialized cell consisting of a single haploid nucleus in a massive and highly ordered cytoplasm whose outer layer (cortex) is obviously distinct. Present in the cytoplasm are numerous yolk droplets which are largely concentrated at the light coloured 'vegetal' pole of the cell (Fig. 1.1). Other cell organelles are distributed unequally along the longitudinal axis of the egg and the nature of the forces which give rise to this polarity constitute the first of the problems posed by embryological analysis. Fertilization of the egg by a sperm triggers an immediate and complex response. A fertilization membrane develops around the egg, which prevents entry of other sperm, fusion of the two haploid nuclei occurs and within about 30 minutes the pigmented cortex rotates with respect to the underlying cytoplasm and in so doing it reveals a grey, crescent shaped area on the side of the egg opposite to the point of entry of the sperm. This is another example of polarity developing. Soon after fertilization the zygote enters a period of rapid nuclear and cell division. The result of this cleavage process is that the egg cytoplasm is partitioned between numerous cells whose ratio of nuclear volume to cytoplasmic volume is more like that found in an 'average' somatic cell. During this cleavage process there is no increase in cell mass, no cell growth, merely an increase in cell number. Thus the polarity impressed on the egg and expressed as an inhomogeneity in the egg cytoplasm becomes transformed, as that cytoplasm is partitioned between the cells of the developing blastula (Fig. 1.1), into a polarity expressed in terms of cell behaviour. The details of the cleavage process and the form of the resulting blastula differ widely depending on the type of egg (and particularily the amount of yolk it contains). In all cases, however, the cells of the blastula eventually cease their rapid division and enter a phase of intensive and profound movements relative to one another. In this process of gastrulation the cells of certain regions (in the case of the frog those that contain the cytoplasm of the grey crescent region) seem to play a key organizing role. The result of the coordinated cell movements of gastrulation (Fig. 1.1) is the formation of layers of cells and axes to the embryo. All the activities of the embryo up to this stage have been at the expense of the food materials stored in the egg but in many organisms, such as the sea urchin, the gastrula develops rapidly into a free-living larva and begins feeding. Even in those organisms where the gastrula is not free-living it is at this stage that the embryo becomes independent of many materials derived from the egg and begins to undertake a number of vital biosynthetic activities for itself. The result of gastrulation is the formation of layers of cells from the relatively formless blastula and the juxtaposition of cells which, in the blastula, were far apart. Such cells can now mutually interact to form structures appropriate to their new positions in the embryo. As a consequence of these interactions, or embryonic inductions as they are called, a particular developmental fate is acquired by the cell which is consequently said to become determined. Each of the layers of cells in the gastrula now gives rise to the appropriate tissues by processes of cell division, cell migration, and cell interaction that seem similar in principle to those occuring during cleavage and gastrulation. The complex of processes which orders the correct determination in space is called pattern formation and the final stage in development occurs when the cells express, at the appropriate time, their final determined status and differentiate into the appropriate cell type. Differentiation involves the construction of the specialized organelles and/or production of specific biochemical end products which characterize and define the hundreds of different cell types of the adult organism. It is thus the last stage in a complex process and although the five features of developing systems which we have identified (polarity, induction, determination, pattern formation and differentiation) can be treated independently, it must never be forgotten that they are components of one continuous process and the distinctions which we draw are for our convenience and not for that of the embryo. Of these five processes four (polarity, determination, pattern formation and induction) are essentially intercellular phenomena which arise as a consequence of cell—cell interactions, whereas cell differentiation is essentially an intracellular phenomenon, involving the interaction of the nucleus and cytoplasm of a single cell. This seems a sensible and useful distinction to make and thus in this book we will deal solely with cell differentiation as defined above and leave the intercellular aspects to be dealt with elsewhere in this series by D.R. Garrod.

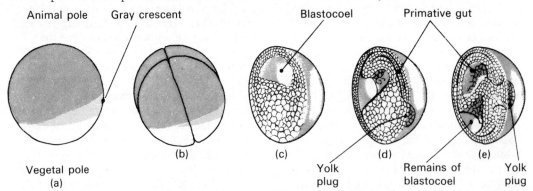

Fig. 1.1 Development of the frog's egg. (a) just after fertilization; (b) 4-cell stage, side view; (c) late blastula; (d) middle gastrulation; (e) late gastrulation. (a, b) whole embroys, (c, d, e) semi-diagrammatic views of sections from the dorsal side or the posterior end. (*after Ebert and Sussex, 1970*)

8

2 Strategy and tactics

There are two possible ways of attempting to understand, experimentally, a complex phenomenon such as cell differentiation. The first, which we may call the reductionist approach, is to break the overall problem down into several smaller problems — much as we have done in the previous section — and then find an animal (or plant) sufficiently simple that it shows only those features necessary for an understanding of each smaller problem. For example, this argument suggests that the bacteriophage (or phage), as the simplest living system (from the chemical point of view) to show the inheritance of mutant characteristics, would be useful for studies of the nature and behaviour of the genetic material and in this case, of course, this reductionist argument has proved tremendously successful.

The alternative approach, which we may call the classical, is more subtle. It assumes that, as a result of intense evolutionary pressures, every conceivable characteristic or possibility inherent in the molecular structure of living organisms will have been exploited and exaggerated by one organism or another. The problem, of course, is to find the organism and recognise the exaggerated feature that it exhibits. As an example of this approach it is believed that the giant polytene chromosomes of the salivary glands of a number of insect larvae represent hundreds or thousands of DNA molecules joined side by side and acting synchronously. If this is true then the observable behaviour of these giant chromosomes accurately reflects the otherwise invisible behaviour of individual DNA molecules, and by studying what polytene chromosomes do we can deduce what happens to DNA molecules both in cells which contain polytene chromosomes and, by analogy, in cells which do not. Similarly the peculiarly low nuclear: cytoplasm ratio of egg cells has necessitated, in a number of instances, special mechanisms for selectively increasing the activity of their ribosomal genes. By studying this one aspect of these otherwise most complicated and complex of cells we may discover the basic rules which govern the expression of all genes — or such is the hope.

These two approaches are complementary; in fact Biology has advanced by first one and then the other of these two philosophies playing the dominant role. Much of the fascination and a lot of the tension of Biological research is in knowing when to use which approach. Unfortunately it is only with hindsight that it is possible to recognise which approach was the most rewarding to use at any one time in the development of a subject — everyone has to use his or her judgement of what is going to pay off in the end.

In this book I am first going to describe some of the simple systems which the reductionists feel are appropriate models for studies of cell differentiation and then having used them to highlight certain problems, examine the systems which the classical approach suggests are ideally suited to answer those problems.

9

3 Model systems, the reductionist approach

3.1 Bacteriophage

The embryological analysis of the frog's egg outlined in the Introduction has shown that cells which are derived from the same cell (the zygote) can do very different things and have very different destinies. All the cells shown in Fig. 1.1 have a past and a future and development is very much concerned with the way the present connects these two. If time is thus the essence of the problem we must ask what is the simplest living system in which a time dependent sequence of well defined and measurable changes occur? The bacteriophages (or phages) seem to fit this specification and in Fig. 3.1. it can be seen that a typical T_{even} phage such as T_2 has a precise and complex structure. The simplicity of the phage lies in its inability to catalyse its own replication unaided. The life cycle of a T_{even} phage (Fig.3.2) starts with the injection of the phage DNA into a bacterial cell (most of the complex structure of Fig.3.1 is concerned with the protection and injection of the DNA). About 30 minutes after infection the host cell bursts and hundreds of mature phage particles are released into the medium to infect other cells. During these 30 minutes, biochemical analysis has shown that a number of novel, phage-specified, enzymic activities appear in the cell and studies of sections cut through infected cells have shown that parallelling this ordered sequence of biochemical events is an ordered sequence of morphological changes. The morphological changes (Fig. 3.2) are a consequence of the ordered sequence of enzymes synthesized and since it is known that these enzymes are synthesized on short-lived messenger RNA (mRNA) molecules [1] the problem posed by Fig. 3.2 is how and why are different mRNA molecules made at different times in the infection process? The phage particle is quite

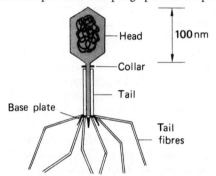

Fig. 3.1 Diagrammatic picture of the structure of a typical T_{even} phage particle. (*after Davidson 1972*)

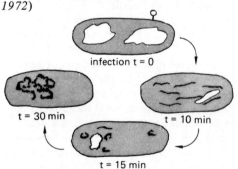

Fig. 3.2 Life cycle of a typical T_{even} phage particle; the white regions are the bacterial DNA, at $t = 10$ min fibrillar phage DNA appears and at $t = 15$ min mature phage particles can be seen.

10

devoid of any enzyme activity including any DNA-primed RNA synthetase (transcriptase) enzyme and so the first RNA molecule made using the injected phage DNA as template must be synthesized using the host enzyme as catalyst. Studies of the detailed enzymology of the *Escherichia coli* enzyme were delayed by its lability and the fact that, as Wood and Berg showed [2], it was possible to have RNA molecules synthesized (using as a measure of the amount of synthesis the incorporation of ^{32}P from nucleotides into macromolecular materials) which were inactive when a biological assay for mRNA (ability to support protein synthesis) was used. In other words it appeared that sometimes the enzyme made biologically meaningful molecules and sometimes it made nonsense molecules. Part of the explanation of this seems to lie in the nature of the DNA — denatured DNA molecules tend to catalyse the synthesis of nonsense RNA — but, when the *E. coli* enzyme was finally purified, it was found that part of the explanation was also due to the complexity of the enzyme molecule itself. Transcriptase was found to consist of two components [3] called the core and the σ-factor (σ = sigma). These two components were quite readily separated by many of the standard procedures for purifying enzymes, thus accounting for the apparent 'lability' of the enzyme. The core component seems to contain the active site of the enzyme since it catalysed the synthesis of macromolecular RNA molecules from DNA preparations of all types, but these molecules were nonsense molecules. The σ-factor was necessary for the synthesis of biologically meaningful molecules. The net effect of adding σ-factor preparations to the core component is thus to suppress the synthesis of nonsense RNA and to modify the catalytic activity of the enzyme so that only certain regions of the DNA are used as a template for RNA synthesis.

The σ-factor has no apparent enzymic

Table 1. Activity of *E. coli* transcriptase.

DNA template	Activity* of	
	core	core + σ
T$_4$ native	0·5	33
T$_4$ denatured	0·5	6·1
Calf thymus native	14·2	32·8
Calf thymus denatured	3·3	14·5

*in arbitrary units. Data from [3].

activity itself (such as a nuclease activity) and appears to act solely as a protein which modifies the activity of another protein — the core. Such modifier proteins or polypeptides are probably common in other systems but their importance is only just beginning to be recognised (see Section 4.5).

In Table 1 it can be seen that T$_4$ DNA is an acceptable template for the *E. coli* enzyme but it was shown that only a few regions of the DNA were in fact transcribed in the presence of the σ-factor [4]. One of the few mRNA molecules made appears to code for a protein which resembles the σ-factor for if transcriptase preparations are now made not from pure *E. coli* cells but from *E. coli* cells infected with T$_4$ phage particles then a different set of regions of the T$_4$ DNA molecules are transcribed into RNA copies. That this explanation is in fact correct was shown by dissociating the two preparations and showing that whereas they had the same core component they had different σ-factors. It is interesting that this σ-factor coded for by the T$_4$ phage appears to modify the *E. coli* core protein so that it recognizes the DNA of T$_{even}$ phages only — it does not stimulate RNA synthesis from other phages such as the λ-phage or the T$_{odd}$ phages. The explanation for the synthesis of different RNA molecules at different times, which underlies Fig. 3.2, thus appears to be that the host transcriptase only transcribes certain regions of the invading DNA. These RNA molecules code for the synthesis (by the host protein synthesising machinery) of those proteins that appear first in the infection

11

cycle, one of which is a σ-factor type of molecule. This phage σ-factor then displaces the *E.coli* σ-factor from combination with the core component, so altering the specificity of the enzyme. This leads to the cessation of the synthesis of the RNA molecules coding for the early functions and initiates the synthesis of RNA molecules which code for proteins which appear later in the infection cycle. This explanation implies that there are specific regions on the DNA which are recognized by the transcriptase and which control where RNA synthesis is initiated. Such regions have been detected, using genetic techniques, in both *E.coli* and phage, and have been called promoter regions. We can imagine therefore, that genes transcribed at the same time have similar promoters and that synthesis of one set of mRNA molecules is switched off simultaneously with switching on another set by the synthesis of the appropriate σ-factor. This is a positive control mechanism in that the σ-factor causes the appearance of a given set of molecules, and must be distinguished from negative control mechanisms (which are also known and are of great significance, p. 14) which prevent the appearance of a given set of molecules. This straightforward picture has been complicated (naturally) by more recent work, and Travers [5] has summarized the burgeoning evidence for the complexity of bacterial transcriptases. It is clear that both the core and the σ-factor components are themselves made up of subunits and that as well as the wholesale replacement of parts of the transcriptase molecule there can be phage specified modifications made of parts of the molecule which are largely conserved. It is also clear that the simple division of the infection cycle into two phases consisting of the early and the late functions is an over-simplification; the early functions have been sub-divided into the immediate-early and the late-early functions for example, but despite these elaborations the basic idea of temporal control of mRNA synthesis by σ-factors with

different promoter specificities has survived.

One of the great attractions of using phage as an experimental system is that they are amenable to very precise and accurate fine structure genetic analysis. However, since the functions which are of interest to developmental biologists are, in general, vital for the survival of the organism, it might be supposed that genetic techniques are of little interest since the mutations which are of interest would be lethal. This is generally true, but in the case of phage and some other organisms, it is possible to obtain 'conditional lethal' mutants which are deficient in a vital function only under some environmental conditions and use these for genetic analysis. Two kinds of conditional lethal mutations have been used, the first and most widely used class, temperature sensitive mutations, arise from the fact that phage development can proceed at 37°C or 42°C. It is possible to obtain mutant phages which can still develop normally at 37°C but which are unable to develop normally at 42°C. In these mutant strains the mutational event is usually such that the amino acid sequence of a vital phage enzyme [6] has been altered in a fashion which affects the temperature stability of the enzyme but which leaves it catalytically active at the lower, or permissive, temperature. The other class of conditional lethal mutations are host range mutations. Wild type phage can grow in a number of different *E.coli* strains despite slight, but significant differences in the way in which different bacterial strains react to foreign DNA, and in the way in which they synthesise proteins. However, it is possible to alter the nucleotide sequence of a phage gene so that whilst it can still function in one strain of *E.coli*, it is ineffective in another. As a result of the analysis of thousands of conditional lethal mutations of these two types, it has been possible to deduce how the various genes are arranged with respect to one another on the phage linkage map (Fig. 3.3). Like the linkage maps of some other phages and bacteria, the T_{even} map is circular and it soon became apparent that related functions tended to be clustered in the same region of the map. Thus all the early functions appeared clustered in the 10-12 o'clock region of the map. Although a number of conditional lethal mutants are incapable of completing their life cycle successfully under the restrictive condition, it was found that a number could carry out part of the cycle, and by correlating such morphological analyses with genetic studies it was found that genes concerned with the synthesis of the same structure also tended to cluster in the same region of the map.

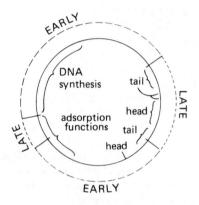

Fig. 3.3 Simplified genetic linkage map of T_{even} phage showing clustering of genes concerned with the synthesis of the same structure.

The number of gene products required for the synthesis of a morphological structure seems often to be rather large. 21 genes are needed, for example, for the synthesis of the tail (Fig. 3.1) although nothing like this number of protein species is actually found in the tail of the mature phage. The conclusion, therefore, seems to be that many of these gene products are in some way concerned with the specification, or assembly, of the multicomponent structure [7]. Since it has recently proved possible to study the synthesis, *in vitro*, of many of the components

of the phage particle by mixing extracts obtained from bacteria infected with different mutants, such predictions can soon be tested directly. If they should prove correct then it would imply that a lot of genetic information is needed to specify morphological structure, and if the same rules that apply to the construction of a phage particle apply to the construction, say, of a nervous system, then an incredible number of 'morphogenetic principles' would seem to be needed.

Thus there appear to be three ideas which stem from this work on the life cycle of the phage:

(1) temporal control of mRNA synthesis may be achieved by alteration of the specificity of the transcriptase enzyme.

(2) genes controlling the same functions may be clustered together in a genetic linkage map — and thus on a DNA molecule. — and

(3) that a lot of genetic material may be needed to specify a structure of complex morphology.

3.2 Enzyme induction in bacteria

It is a little confusing that the two operationally distinct phenomena of embryonic induction and enzyme induction should have similar names. The reason is that it has long been hoped that there is a similar fundamental cause underlying them both and many of those who began the modern work on the phenomena made no bones about using bacteria as a model system for studying embryogenesis. The first system to be fully analysed was the induction of β-galactosidase in *E. coli* K12. A vast amount is now known about this system; an entire book was recently published devoted to just this topic [8] and most standard textbooks contain a diagram of the type shown in Fig. 3.4 which derives from the initial diagram published by Jacob and Monod in their classic paper [9]. A full account of the evidence which has given rise to Fig. 3.4

13

can be found in [10], but briefly the situation may be summarized by stating that:

(1) The genetic region controlling the appearance of β-galactosidase activity in *E.coli* contains three structural genes specifying the amino acid sequences of the β-galactosidase protein itself (z-gene), a permease (i.e. a protein concerned in the uptake) for β-galactosides (y-gene), and a transacetylase whose physiological function is still uncertain (a-gene).

(2) The activity of these three structural genes is coordinately controlled by three other genetic elements.

(3) One of these elements — the i-gene — is the structural gene for a regulatory protein, the repressor, which is capable of binding both low molecular weight compounds (inducers) and binding to a region of the DNA immediately next to the z-gene called the operator or o-gene. When the repressor binds an inducer molecule it is unable to bind to the operator region and conversely, when it is free of inducer it binds to the DNA.

(4) The promoter region, where the transcriptase enzyme first binds to the DNA, is in turn, adjacent to the operator and the transcriptase is only capable of moving along the DNA strand and so of initiating transcription at the z-gene when the repressor is not binding to the operator.

(5) The whole complex of elements, i, p, o, z, y, a is known as an 'operon' or, more precisely, the lac operon, since the physiologically significant substrate for β-galactosidase is lactose.

The evidence for the scheme described in Fig. 3.4 is largely genetic and comes from the analysis, in particular, of mutants which make β-galactosidase in the absence of inducers or never make it at all. Such mutants clearly have defects in the regulatory elements of the

operon and the fine structure mapping and complementation analysis of such mutants defines the elements i, p and o. Similar studies have been done with other operons of *E.coli*, in particular those involved in the catabolism of arabinose and the biosynthesis of tryptophan, histidine and arginine. In the biosynthetic systems it is found that the presence of the end product of the pathway is necessary for the repressor to bind to the operator and thus prevent transcription of the structural genes for the biosynthetic enzymes. In this sense the low molecular weight end products of biosynthetic pathways act in exactly the opposite sense to the way in which inducers of catabolic enzymes act. Detailed analysis of these other systems [10, 11] has shown that they also differ in other respects from the lac operon, representing in many instances considerable elaborations of the simple scheme shown in Fig. 3.4. However, in principle it is clear that with a suitable combination of positive control elements (such as the σ-factor/promoter) and negative elements (such as the repressor/operator system) it is possible to devise theoretical schemes of virtually endless complexity which can account for many of the cases of altered protein synthesis seen during development. This has been done [12] but in the absence of systems of genetic analysis of much greater precision than those available at present for higher organisms, it seems that such schemes must remain hypothetical.

It has been recognized for many years that the ability of many bacterial operons to respond to their controlling systems was quantitatively

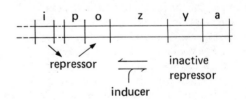

Fig. 3.4 Regulation of the lac operon

14

dependent on the metabolic state of the cell. For example, inducers of β-galactosidase are less effective in eliciting β-galactosidase synthesis when *E. coli* is growing in media containing glucose than when it is growing in media containing glycerol. Such effects seem to be mediated via alterations in the level of a compound, 3′, 5′-cyclic AMP (or cAMP), whose level reflects the nutritional status of the cell. *E. coli* cells contain a cAMP binding protein and this protein, when bound to cAMP, appears to assist in the function of the promoter region of the lac operon.

Studies of enzyme induction in bacteria have thus clarified ideas of how protein synthesis might be controlled and in particular:

(1) have established criteria whereby control elements acting at the DNA level may be recognized, and

(2) have shown that as well as qualitative, on/off switches of various kinds, mechanisms exist to alter, quantitatively, the extent to which a given gene is active.

3.3 Spore formation and germination in bacteria

All the proteins of an operon are regulated coordinately, that is to say either all of them or none of them are synthesised at any one time. In a differentiating system, however, what is observed is a time-dependent change in the pattern of protein synthesis and so attempts have been made to find a bacterial system in which this aspect of the developing system would also be observed. Advantage could then be taken of the sophisticated genetic techniques available to study the way in which this time dependence can be added to the control systems discussed in the previous section. There are two kinds of system which are attractive in this context. The first is, in a sense, so obvious that it is often overlooked. A bacterium has a definite morphology and when it replicates it seems obvious that its components must be synthesised and assembled to form this

morphology in a precisely controlled and integrated fashion. Thus studies of the events which occur as a young bacterium grows and divides, should reveal a time-dependent sequence of events just as precise as that sequence which we know occurs during the replication of a phage particle. It is possible to obtain cultures of bacteria which grow in a highly synchronous fashion where every bacterium is doing exactly the same as every other one, and studies of such cultures [13] have shown that there is indeed a time dependent sequence of changes in macromolecular syntheses upon which the type of controls discussed in Section 3.2 is superimposed. However, such studies have not progressed to the point where we understand how the time dependence is achieved.

Some bacteria, especially the *Bacilli* and *Clostridia*, also undergo another type of time dependent sequence which is much more immediately recognizable as being analogous to differentiation in higher organisms. These bacteria can, under some environmental conditions, form spores which are very different in morphology and metabolic activity from the normal vegetative cell. Under the appropriate conditions, which usually involve severe depletion of the usable carbon sources for growth, if not outright starvation, the individual cells in a culture will sporulate synchronously, with a highly regulated and tightly coupled series of changes in protein synthesis and morphology (Fig. 3.5). Since sporulation takes place in the absence of optimal exogenous sources of energy and biosynthetic intermediates, one of the first of these changes involves the appearance of new hydrolytic enzymes and the rapid degradation of much of the vegatative cell. The nutrients so generated are then reassembled to form spore specific products. It seems clear that the transcriptase enzyme of the vegetative cell is one of the many vegatative functions to be modified, since the phage ϕe will only replicate in a vegetative cell and ϕe DNA is not a suitable template

15

for transcriptase preparations from sporulating cells [14]. Similarly the aldolase of the vegetative cell is modified by protease action to form that aldolase characteristic of the spore [15]. Thus in these cases it seems as if the loss or modification of an enzyme or activity can be as significant an event as is the acquisition of a novel enzyme or activity in the overall differentiation process.

Many attempts have been made to find when the vegetative cell becomes irreversibly 'committed' to sporulation — since such a commitment would be analogous to the process of determination discussed in the Introduction. Some such studies [16] have suggested that rather than there being a unique point in time at which the cell becomes committed it becomes committed to the various definable stages in the overall process (Fig. 3.5) in sequence, each commitment step probably representing the synthesis of an appropriate species of mRNA; since commitment to an event, and the ability of the cell to carry out that event in the presence of actinomycin D (a drug which inhibits transcription), occur virtually simultaneously. Commitment to an event precedes that event by about an hour, and so the implication of this is that the half life of mRNA molecules in the sporulating cell is much longer than is the half life of the average mRNA in the vegetative cell (which is usually about 2—10 minutes), and this despite the appearance in the sporulating cell of an enhanced RNAase activity. These studies of commitment and mRNA stability have not gone uncriticised: for an alternative interpretation see [17].

The germination of a bacterial spore (a matter of considerable economic importance) provides a similar time dependent sequence of events which, since large populations of spores can be induced to germinate synchronously, is experimentally attractive. However, little has been added by such studies which is conceptually new.

Thus, two new ideas have been contributed to our discussion of cell differentiation by these studies on bacterial sporulation:

(1) loss of an ability to carry out a process can be as significant an event in differentiation as is the acquisition of the ability to carry out a novel process, and

(2) that mRNA molecules can have very different half lives in the same cell at different times and that therefore there must be control mechanisms which act at points after transcription, but before the fully active protein molecules are formed.

3.4 Are prokaryotes good models for eukaryotes?
Whilst all living organisms are, at the molecular/biochemical level astonishingly similar there are nevertheless important and fundamental differences between prokaryotes (bacteria and the blue-green algae) on the one hand and the eukaryotes (all other cells) on the other. Not the least of these differences is that the complex cell differentiation, so typical of eukaryote organisms, usually occurs as the end result of a complex series of intercellular interactions, whilst amongst the prokaryotes cell differentiation is usually an intracellular phenomenon. Thus, whereas it is easy to find amongst prokaryotes examples of time-dependent differentiation, it is not so common, or easy, to find examples of the spatial differentiation typical of, say, an embryo. There are also, of course, very real differences between these two classes of cell at the molecular/biochemical level as well as similarities.

In Fig. 3.6 the typical features of prokaryotes and eukaryotes are summarized. For a beautifully illustrated and authoritative summary of modern cytological work see [18]. Apart from the very different sizes of the two cells in Fig. 3.6 (a bacterium is approximately the size of a mitochondrion) the most obvious difference is the complex system of membranes and membrane

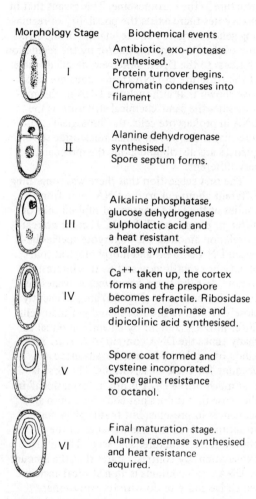

Morphology	Stage	Biochemical events
	I	Antibiotic, exo-protease synthesised. Protein turnover begins. Chromatin condenses into filament
	II	Alanine dehydrogenase synthesised. Spore septum forms.
	III	Alkaline phosphatase, glucose dehydrogenase sulpholactic acid and a heat resistant catalase synthesised.
	IV	Ca^{++} taken up, the cortex forms and the prespore becomes refractile. Ribosidase adenosine deaminase and dipicolinic acid synthesised.
	V	Spore coat formed and cysteine incorporated. Spore gains resistance to octanol.
	VI	Final maturation stage. Alanine racemase synthesised and heat resistance acquired.

Fig. 3.5 Morphological and biochemical events associated with sporulation in *Bacillus* spp. Redrawn from [16].

bound organelles present in the eukaryote cell. Since it is known that transport of materials across membranes is a closely regulated process [19], this means that the eukaryote cell can maintain within itself compartments in which mutually incompatible reactions can be contained and exploited. Some of these organelles, such as the mitochondrion and the chloroplast, contain DNA and are thus, to a limited extent, even genetically autonomous. This greater morphological complexity does not imply a greater biochemical capacity, however; on the contrary, from a purely biochemical point of view a bacterium such as *E.coli* or a *Pseudomonad* is far more versatile than is Man, and can catalyse many more different chemical reactions. What the eukaryote cell can do, though, is to control and thus exploit its more limited chemical repertoire more effectively. The problem posed by cell differentiation is not, primarily, a problem of discovering novel chemical reactions, but rather it is a problem of discovering how ubiquitous reactions can be controlled differently in different cells and in the same cell at different times. One implication of this, of course, is that prokaryotes may lack precisely those controls which are of most significance for cell differentiation in higher organisms. It is probably significant that those prokaryotes which show the most complex patterns of cell differentiation, (including some simple intercellular effects) the *Bacilli*, *Actinomycetes* and blue-green algae [20], have the most highly developed internal membrane systems amongst the prokaryotes.

The other major difference between the cells in Fig 3.6 is in the way in which they handle their DNA. In prokaryotes there is no nucleus and the DNA consists of a single molecule, often circular, which is not in any obvious way associated with any other cellular component (except perhaps the cell membrane). In eukaryote cells, in complete contrast, the DNA is enclosed in organelles, and in one organelle, the nucleus, the DNA is associated with considerable

17

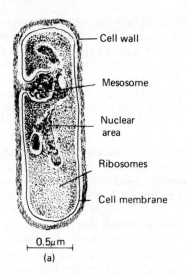

Cell wall

Mesosome

Nuclear
area

Ribosomes

Cell membrane

|— 0.5μm —|

(a)

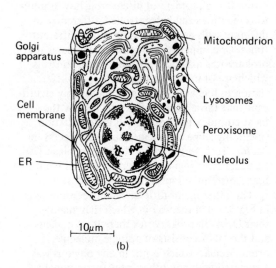

Golgi
apparatus

Cell
membrane

ER

Mitochondrion

Lysosomes

Peroxisome

Nucleolus

|— 10μm —|

(b)

Fig. 3.6 Diagram of the ultrastructure of (a) a typical prokaryote (*Bacillus*) and (b) a typical eukaryote (mammalian liver) cell, (*after Novikoff and Holtzman, 1970*)

18

amounts of protein and RNA to form another structure — the chromosome. This means that in eukaryotes there exists the possibility of regulating gene activity by the regulation of the structure of the chromosome and/or by the regulation of access to the DNA. Moreover, detailed studies of the structure of DNA from eukaryote cells have shown that although the DNA in chromosomes has the same chemical structure as the DNA in prokaryote cells, the 'biological' structure that is the way in which nucleotide sequences are distributed along the molecule, is very different.

The first suggestion that there was something different about eukaryote DNA came from studies of the DNA content of diploid cells of different organisms (Table 2). There is no real correlation amongst the eukaryote species between DNA content and morphological complexity or evolutionary status. It is interesting to note that the two *Chironomous* species discussed in Section 4.1.2 (p. 38) are sufficiently closely related to interbreed and yet their cells differ in DNA content by an amount equal to many times the DNA content of *E. coli*. Two kinds of explanation can be advanced to account for these observations. The first is that much of the DNA is not 'informational' in the sense that it does not code for amino acid sequences in proteins, but that it plays some structural role in the maintenance of the chromosome structure. The second kind of explanation, by contrast, states that the amount of DNA a cell contains is an historical accident which has more to do with its evolutionary history than any chemical or biochemical aspect of chromosome function [21]. These two explanations are not mutually exclusive, and persuasive arguments have been advanced for both of them.

That much of the DNA of eukaryotes is not informational is suggested first by the fact that the DNA content of mouse cells is sufficient to code for at least 1000 times the number of proteins that have been found, so far, in mice.

It seems inconceivable that there are that number of proteins that have escaped detection – although we cannot be sure how many might be needed to build morphologically complex structures. Secondly, there is direct experimental evidence that not all the DNA can code for protein molecules. The density of a DNA molecule is a function of its guanine and cytosine content and is in the range 1.6–1.8 g/ml. Solutions of CsCl and $CsSO_4$ can be obtained which cover this range of density and thus the G + C content

Table 2. Relative DNA contents of cells of various species.

Species	Relative DNA Content
T$_{even}$ bacteriophage*	0·00006
*E.coli.**	0·0014
Fungus (yeast)*	0·007
(*Dictyostelium discoideum*)*	0·04
Fly (*Drosophila*)	0·046
Tunicate (*Ciona intestinalis*)	0·056
Coelenterate (*Cassiopeia*)	0·096
Echinoderm (*Lytechinus pictus*)	0·26
Toad (*Xenopus*)	0·86
Mouse (*Mus musculus*)	1·00**
Frog (*Rana pipiens*)	13
Lungfish (*Lepidosiren paradoxa*)	35·4

*haploid cell, all other figures are for diploid cells.
**(1·00 = 7×10^{-12} g DNA).

of a DNA can be determined from a knowledge of the position at which it comes to rest in a density gradient made from these salts. When high molecular weight DNA preparations from eukaryote cells are thus analysed, broad bands, indicative of a wide range of base compositions amongst the molecules, are obtained. Frequently shoulders, or even discrete peaks, of much lower height than the main band of DNA can also be seen. The 'satellite' bands (Fig. 3.7) can represent DNA from the mitochondria (or chloroplasts) but in some species even DNA prepared from nuclei will contain satellites of this kind. If the DNA preparations

are sheared so that the average molecular weight of the molecules decreases then these bands sharpen and the nuclear satellite bands become more prominent and they can be isolated and characterized. Such a study of the nuclear α-satellite of the guinea-pig has shown that it has a very simple chemical structure consisting of the nucleotide sequence:

5′–CCCTAA–3′
3′–GGGATT–5′

repeated many times [22]. Although a bacterial DNA primed RNA polymerase can use this DNA as a template for making RNA no protein molecules have been detected with the amino acid sequence which would result from the use of this kind of RNA molecule as an mRNA. However, the use of purified satellite DNA as an *in vitro* template does enable the highly radioactive RNA transcripts to be used as histological reagents for locating those base sequences in the chromosomes which are complementary to them i.e. the satellite DNA. In principle this elegant technique consists of fixing a cell to a slide, heating it to melt the DNA (i.e. separate the two strands of the double helices) and then incubating the slide at a lower temperature in the presence of the RNA to allow formation of RNA–DNA hybrids and, of course, reformation of DNA–DNA double helices. The slide can now be stained (to locate the DNA) and autoradiographed (to locate the RNA) and the position of the satellite DNA is thus visualized. Using this technique it has been shown that the nuclear satellite DNA is localized predominantly at the centromeres of the chromosomes although a little also appears to be scattered throughout the chromosome where there are heterochromatic regions. (see Section 4.1.3) [23].

All chromosomes have centromeres and this work suggests that even those organisms which do not have obvious nuclear satellites might, in fact, have similar molecules but with a G + C content that precludes their being separated in a density gradient from the bulk of the DNA.

19

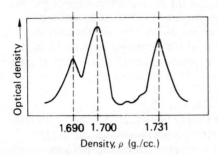

Fig. 3.7 Density gradient analysis of mouse DNA showing nuclear satellite ($\rho = 1 \cdot 69$), main band ($\rho = 1 \cdot 70$) and marker DNA from *Micrococcus* ($\rho = 1 \cdot 731$).

Analysis of the concentration of base sequences in a DNA preparation by reannealing experiments suggests that this is in fact so. In these experiments DNA molecules are sheared so that each is approximately the same size and the molecules are then melted. This causes a detectable change in the light absorption at 260nm and in the behaviour of the molecules on an hydroxyapatite column. The melted DNA preparation is then incubated at a temperature below its melting temperature so that the double helices may reform and the rate at which this reformation or reannealing occurs can be detected by measurements of the OD_{260nm} or behaviour on hydroxyapatite. Many factors will affect the rate of this reaction, such as the base composition of the DNA, the ionic strength of the medium and the temperature at which reannealing occurs, but if all these are kept constant and allowed for, these rates can be used as a measure of the relative concentration, in the DNA, of various base sequences. Single strands of DNA present which have been derived from sequences present in multiple copies (say a million or so) will obviously find a complementary partner much faster than will single strands

20

of DNA derived from sequences present in only one copy. Very wide variations in rates of reannealing are found which is interpreted as reflecting wide variations in the concentrations of various base sequence in the DNA. The experiments are usually summarized by plotting the percentage of reannealing against the C_0t (pronounced 'cot') where C_0 is the initial concentration of DNA and t is the time (in seconds) taken to achieve a given percentage of reanealing. Such C_0t curves (Fig. 3.8) can be interpreted in terms of relative amounts of base sequences as shown in Fig. 3.9 [24].

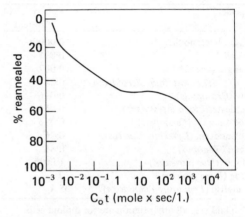

Fig. 3.8 Kinetics of reannealing of mouse DNA Redrawn from [24].

The nuclear satellite of mouse corresponds to the 10% of highly repetitious or reiterated DNA which comprise a family of molecules sufficiently homogenous and present in sufficiently high relative concentration to give a discrete peak in the density gradient analysis. Not all organisms have such a large amount of DNA with this degree of reiteration but all eukaryotes have DNA with some highly repetitious sequences. sequences.

The differences that we have discussed so far between prokaryotes and eukaryotes (Fig. 3.6) have all been differences in structure. There are also, as might be expected, differences in dynamic behaviour, and and in particular in the way in which various events which occur in the cell cycle are distributed within it [13]. A prokaryote cell usually contains just one molecule of DNA whose replication thus represents a unique as well as a uniquely important event. This replication does not, however, seem to be very directly linked with the cell division cycle. In fact the rate of replication of DNA in *E.coli* B/r takes a constant time (40 min) irrespective of changes in doubling time which vary over the range 20–60 min. The fact that doubling times can be faster than the rate of synthesis of a DNA molecule means that in order to ensure that all daughter cells have a complete genome further rounds of replication must be initiated before completion of the first. This means that a bacterial cell will contain a different ratio of genes near the initiation point for DNA synthesis to genes far from the initiation point at different rates of growth. This situation is inconceivable in eukaryotes where the process of cell division must be preceded by the orderly and complete separation of the two daughter chromosome sets in mitosis or meosis (during which time DNA synthesis is impossible). Thus the cell cycle in eukaryotes (Fig. 3.10) must always have a distinct S phase when DNA synthesis occurs separated by periods (the G or gap phases and mitosis) when DNA synthesis does not occur. This also means that eukaryote cells will have a more closely controlled number of genes and probably, that different criteria will be significant for ordering the genes on the linkage map with respect to the initiation point for DNA synthesis. A further implication of the precision with which the cell cycle is regulated in eukaryotes is that there must be a close coupling between the controls which regulate cell differentiation and those which regulate the cell cycle.

Embryonic cells usually divide very quickly

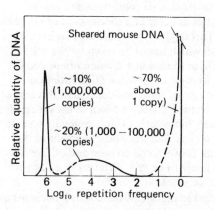

Fig. 3.9 Frequency of repetition of nucleotide sequences in mouse DNA (dashed segments represent regions of uncertainty) Redrawn from [24].

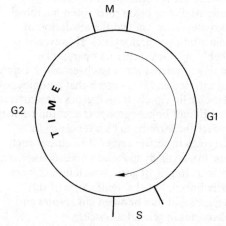

Fig. 3.10 The eukaryote cell cycle.

and have a very short or even no G1 = G'one' phase. Cells from older embryos have longer doubling times, due largely to an increase in the length of the G1 phase. It was at one time thought that cell differentiation and growth were mutually exclusive phenomena but this is now known not to be necessarily true. It is true,

21

however, that differentiated cells often do not divide under normal conditions and can be thought of as being in a special kind of G1 phase $- G_0$. This implies that there is some kind of decision which has to be taken by the cell to enter G_0 or remain in a division orientated G1 phase. In some cells whose differentiation phenomena are hormone-dependent it seems as if this decision might be taken in the preceeding G2 phase, but whether this is generally true or not, it is clear that the whole problem of the coupling between cell division and differentiation is likely to be very different in eukaryotes and prokaryotes.

A marked feature of the control mechanisms of prokaryotes is that genes with a similar or metabolically related function are often found clustered in the same region of genetic linkage maps, if not actually adjacent as are the z, y and a genes of the lac operon. Unfortunately genetic studies of eukaryotes (even microbial eukaryotes) have not had the resolution of similar studies of prokaryotes. However, it is probably significant that no operon-like grouping of related genes has been convincingly demonstrated and it is known that a number of metabolically closely related genes are scattered over different linkage groups (i.e. chromosomes) — in fact there seems to be a tendency in eukaryotes to scatter rather than cluster such genes. Interestingly in *Pseudomonads* there is a similar scattering of genes which in *E. coli* are closely linked, but the significance of this difference and that between eukaryotes and prokaryotes in general is obscure.

Thus there are very real differences between prokaryote and eukaryote cells:

(1) in cell structure and compartmentation
(2) in the detailed structure of the nuclear DNA and the way in which this DNA is organized (or not organized) to form chromosomes
(3) in coupling between cell division, cell differentiation and other events in the cell cycle, and
(4) in the arrangement of genes on the linkage groups.

Of course, at the most fundamental levels of molecular and biochemical structure there remain great similarities and only time will tell whether it is more important for a study of cell differentiation to emphasize the similarities or the differences.

3.5 The cellular slime mould *Dictyostelium discoideum*

One complication recognized in the preceeding section was that cell division and cell differentiation must be intimately connected processes. This connection is not only a considerable theoretical problem but it is also quite a technical nuisance for it is often difficult to distinguish between events which are really a consequence of differentiation and those which are a consequence of the cell cycle when both sets of events are occurring simultaneously. These difficulties make the cellular slime mould particularly attractive because in the life cycle of this organism growth and cell differentiation are mutually exclusive phenomena. Whether in deciding to view this organism as a model system for higher organisms we have consequently discarded the baby with the bath water, of course, remains an open question and one which can be asked of any reductionist approach.

The amoebae of *D. discoideum* are found in bacteria-rich soils where they are indistinguishable from other soil amoebae. They feed on bacteria and will continue to grow and divide indefinitely whilst provided with food. When, however, their food runs out and if they are on a solid surface (as they are in the soil) then their behaviour changes dramatically. The amoebae converge about a central point forming a macroscopic aggregate. The aggregate (Fig. 3.11) is a tissue-like entity which can contain up to 40,000 cells. The first cells to arrive at the centre of the aggregate become elevated above the substratum

22

by the subsequent arrival of others and so a finger-like projection is formed which falls over on its side and begins to migrate. The migration phase (grex) can be omitted altogether from the sequence or indefinitely extended depending on the environmental conditions. In the soil, however, it seems clear from the way in which the grex responds to light, humidity, and temperature, that the grex would move to the surface and there construct the fruiting body whose formation represents the end and the point of the cell differentiation phase. The fruiting body consists of a slender cylindrical stalk containing cellulose encased stalk cells and bearing aloft a mass of spore cells. These cells are encased in a thick cell

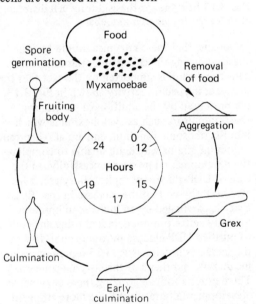

Fig. 3.11 Life cycle of the cellular slime mould *D. discoideum*. The times refer to development on Millipore filters. Redrawn from [26].

wall of polysaccharide material which protects them from dessication. In the soil, rain would distribute the spores to other parts of the soil where, if bacteria are present, the spores germi-

nate, each giving rise to one amoeboid cell and thus completing the cycle. The ecological rationale for this behaviour in terms of dispersal seems convincing but one of the chief attractions of this organism as a model system for studying cell differentiation, is that differentiation is initiated by the withdrawl of food. Thus all growth related phenomena occur in the vegetative phase and so do not confuse the differentiation studies. The pattern of cell differentiation is simple, involving only three cell types (Fig. 3.12), yet sufficiently complex to possess features which appear analogous to those occurring during embryogenesis. The cells in the grex have to decide to become *either* spore cells *or* stalk cells and in this sense there is obviously cell—cell interaction involved since the choices are ordered in space in such a manner that a fruiting body results. Thus as well as temporal differentiation in *D. discoideum* we also have a simple example of spatial differentiation [25]. A final argument for studying this organism is that although there appears to be no obligatory coupling of genetic recombination to the cell differentiation, a parasexual system of genetic recombination does appear to occur and thus in this organism there is the hope (since the amoebae are haploid with only seven chromosomes) of successfully applying the methods of prokaryote microbial genetics.

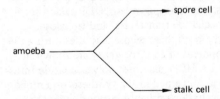

Fig. 3.12 Cell differentiation in *D. discoideum*.

Since the amoebae are haploid it is easy to obtain mutant strains which are conditionally lethal (most usefully temperature sensitive) just as in the case of phage. Three types of temperature-sensitive mutant have been described (Table 3) corresponding to lesions in genes

23

specifically required for growth (GTS), or differentiation (DTS), or in genes required during both phases of the life cycle (TS). Genetic analysis of these mutants has only just begun — it is not yet known if they are grouped together

Table 3. Temperature-sensitive mutant strains of *D. discoideum* (after Loomis).

Strain*	Growth at 27°	Differentiation at 27°
wild type	+	+
GTS	−	+
DTS	+	−
TS	−	−

*all strains grow and differentiate normally at 22°

in any way — but the fact that DTS mutants exist implies that during the differentiation processes genes are activated and thus we are dealing here, as in the other cases discussed, with cell differentiation occurring as a result of differential gene activation. Direct evidence for the differential activation of genes during differentiation has come from studies of the synthesis of new enzymes during the formation of the fruiting body. The fruiting body contains many polysaccharides not present in the amoebae and so many studies have been concerned with enzymes involved in various aspects of polysaccharide synthesis. Three such enzymes are UDP-glucose pyrophosphorylase, UDP-galactose: polysaccharide transferase, and trehalose-6-phosphate synthase whose activities during the development of *D. discoideum* are shown in Fig. 3.13. UDP-galactose: polysaccharide transferase is concerned in the synthesis of a mucopolysaccharide probably responsible for the spores in the spore mass sticking together, trehalose is the characteristic storage material of the spore and UDP-glucose pyrophosphorylase catalyses the synthesis of UDP-glucose (from UTP and glucose-l-phosphate) from which other carbohydrates are in turn synthesized. It is thus

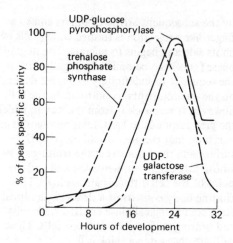

Fig. 3.13 Enzyme synthesis during cell differentiation of *D. discoideum* amoebae.

reasonable that these enzymes should be synthesized during the cell differentiation process. This conclusion is supported by the fact that the increases in specific activity shown in Fig. 3.13, are prevented by the addition of protein synthesis inhibitors such as cycloheximide which inhibits ribosome function, and are also aberrant in mutant strains which are unable to complete the developmental process successfully. In the case of UDP-glucose pyrophosphorylase, it has also been shown that the increase in specific activity is parallelled by an increase in immunologically active protein detected using antibodies to purified UDP-glucose pyrophosphorylase so the increases noted in Fig. 3.13 represent genuine *de novo* synthesis of the enzyme concerned. These criteria for categorizing these enzymes as 'developmentally regulated' are more stringent than in many other cases of supposedly developmentally regulated enzyme synthesis but even so it is not certain that they are sufficient. Recently it has been possible to grow the amoebae in a variety of different media thus causing a variety of chemical and enzymic changes in their composition, and study of the subsequent differentiation of these amoebae has shown that alterations in the kinetics of synthesis of some supposedly developmentally regulated enzymes can ensue. However, such changes in growth media do not cause changes in the synthesis of the enzymes shown in Fig. 3.13 and so in these cases the correlation of enzyme synthesis and developmental stage seems valid. It is clear, however, that it might not always be a simple matter to distinguish between those events which are necessarily involved in the progressive changes of morphology which define cell differentiation, and other events which also alter as a consequence of the altered environment and interactions imposed on the cells by the morphogenesis but which are not directly connected with it. In other words it might not always be easy to distinguish causes from effects.

Studies of the effect of inhibitors of RNA synthesis such as actinomycin D on the appearance of the enzymes shown in Fig. 3.13 has suggested that in all three cases there is a requirement for the synthesis of a specific RNA molecule some time before the appearance of the first increase in enzyme activity. It is tempting to call this the mRNA molecule for the enzyme concerned but it is as well to remember that in this, as in many other instances where similar studies of the effects of inhibitors on enzyme synthesis have been carried out, all that has been shown is the requirement for an RNA molecule; which could be a ribosomal component or be involved in some way in mRNA stabilization or transport rather than being a specific mRNA molecule itself. The significant point about these studies, however, is that different times of sensitivity to actinomycin D were found in the three cases (Fig. 3.14) and thus there must exist some regulatory mechanism which operates at the post-transcriptional stages of protein synthesis.

These experiments are, in principle, titration experiments in which enzyme activity appearing subsequent to actinomycin D addition, is used

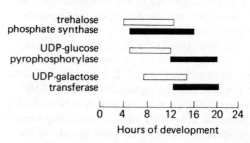

Fig. 3.14 Periods of RNA (□) and protein (■) synthesis required for the appearance of enzyme activities during cell differentiation in *D. discoideum*.

as a measure of specific RNA synthesis prior to actinomycin D addition. Such experiments can only work if there is some strict arithmetic relationship between the RNA and the protein. If there were no such relationship then it would be possible for the cells to compensate for their underproduction of RNA by increasing the efficiency of utilisation of the few RNA molecules that they do posess at the time of drug addition. We have no idea of how such control might operate.

A further feature of these experiments which is of general interest is that addition of actinomycin D at times after 16h gave, not 100% of the enzyme activity, but consistently more than this figure. This 'paradoxical' effect of actinomycin D has been found in a number of other systems where similar experiments have been done and implies that the loss of enzyme activity also depends on prior synthesis of a specific RNA. This means that the loss of a function is probably as significant and controlled an event as is the acquisition of that function.

The situation in the slime mould thus appears to be similar to that in the prokaryotes discussed previously. A complex sequence of morphogenetic events is controlled at the molecular/biochemical level by an array of transcriptional and translational controls. This interpretation has been challenged, however, and it is interesting to see how a completely different interpretation can be put on the sequence of events shown in Fig. 3.12.

The first stage in the life cycle aggregation, (Fig. 3.11), involves the chemotactic movement of cells to a central point. This movement is due to the centre of the aggregate secreting cAMP and establishing a gradient in this substance [27]. If amoebae are placed on agar containing a high concentration of cAMP at a cell density so low that they cannot form aggregates, then the individual cells will, in isolation, form cells which look like stalk cells [28]. It is claimed that this process is insensitive to cycloheximide and actinomycin D and this implies that cAMP can so alter the metabolic behaviour of the amoebae that they can, without synthesizing any novel enzymes, construct stalk cells. Differentiation-specific genetic information would only be required, therefore, for the construction of spore cells and (presumably) for determining the correct morphogenesis.

Wright and her colleagues [29] have gone further and pointed out that the usual rationale for expecting to find *de novo* enzyme synthesis during differentiation, namely that an increased metabolic flux is needed through some pathways so that the cell's function is changed, is open to challenge. They point out that this argument is only valid if the concentration of enzyme is the rate-limiting parameter in the overall metabolic flux. In the cell enzyme concentrations (at least for enzymes such as those of Fig. 3.13) are usually of the order $10^{-5}M$. Substrate and metabolite concentrations are usually of this order too which means that it is just as likely, if not more likely, for the rate limiting factor in the overall metabolic flux to be the enzyme activity which is controlled by substrate or, more generally, metabolite concentrations. Starting from this point Wright has elaborated

26

a kinetic theory of cell differentiation which accounts for the synthesis of novel carbohydrates during the cell differentiation in terms of the changes in size of the pools of a few key metabolites. Starvation and cAMP then control differentiation by initiating a time-dependent sequence of changes in pool sizes, and alterations in the transcriptional and translational controls are now a consequence, and not the cause of these changes in metabolites. That both types of control operate seems clear enough [26], but that either can be said to be the exclusive 'explanation' of cell differentiation seems unlikely. It seems more reasonable to assume that interactions must exist between the control mechanisms which operate at the level of enzyme concentration, and those which operate at the level of enzyme activity. The difficulty is simply one of finding a system in which to investigate these interactions. The complexity of the problem is illustrated by work done recently on the control of trehalose synthesis. In these experiments one lot of amoebae were grown in the presence of glucose and another lot were grown in its absence. The glucose content of the growth medium is known to alter the glycogen content of the amoebae. The amount of trehalose synthesized by each lot of amoebae during their differentiation (which seems little affected by the initial level of glycogen in the amoebae) was then measured. A dramatic difference in the amount of trehalose formed by the two lots of cells was observed (Fig. 3.15). Simultaneous measurements of the amount of trehalose-6-phosphate synthase, trehalase (which degrades trehalose) and several metabolites showed that there was no difference between the two lots of cell in enzyme content, but there were alterations in the level of glucose-6-phosphate and UDP-glucose. However, these alterations were not compatible with the kinetic theory [29]. Clearly the amount of trehalose formed by the cells is controlled by the activity of trehalose-6-phosphate synthase and, equally clearly, the

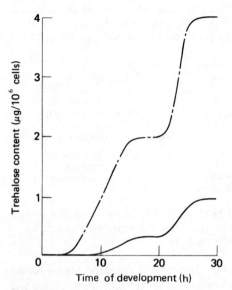

Fig. 3.15

concentration of this enzyme, in the cell, is not controlled by the use the cell is going to make of it in trehalose synthesis. We will have to return to what factors, apart from flux changes, might regulate enzyme activities later (Section 4.6).

Work on the cellular slime mould has thus shown:

(1) that the loss of functions is as significant a process as is the gain of functions for cell differentiation

(2) that transcriptional and translational controls are significant in the differentiation of eukaryotes as well as prokaryotes

(3) that significant controls operating on the activity of enzymes of key metabolic significance for the differentiation process exist, and

(4) that controls operating at one level do not seem to be simply related to those operating at another. The key problem posed by cell differentiation seems likely to be the nature of the interactions between various levels of control.

3.6 Tissue culture cells.

A number of tissues from an adult (or better embryonic) organism can be dissociated into their component cells by incubation with proteolytic enzymes such as trypsin. The cells so produced will often divide a number of times if placed in a suitable medium. Usually after a number of such divisions (usually 60-90) however, most of the cells seem to die and the culture becomes 'taken over' by cells of an altered chromosomal type and/or number and these cells can now continue to divide more or less indefinitely. These facts have been interpreted as showing that each cell in an organism has a finite life span (in terms of the number of divisions it may undergo) and that cell death is an inevitable and programmed event. However, the precise physiological environment of the cells in the intact organism is unknown and thus irreproducible and the fact that many primary cultures undergo a 'crisis' may merely mean that they have run out of some essential compound of which we know nothing. The fact that nevertheless cell cultures can be established is thus more a tribute to the adaptability of living cells than to our ingenuity. There have recently been reports of tissue culture cells growing indefinitely in culture without going through a 'crisis' and possessing normal chromosome complements [30]. The history of cell culture techniques is full of instances where observations have subsequently been shown to be due to an inadequate medium. Thus it was believed that differentiated cells could not be established in culture, and that cell differentiation and cell growth were mutually exclusive phenomena in higher organisms as well as in the cellular slime mould. This belief stemmed from the fact that the only cells that seemed to survive the 'division crisis' were

';undifferentiated' fibroblast type cells. We now know, however, that such cells are less exacting in their nutritive requirements than are most differentiated cells and thus will be selected for in inadequate media. If suitable media are provided then we know that a variety of differentiated cell types including muscle [31] and cartilage [32] can be cloned and maintained in culture and there express their differentiated function(s). In the case of the embryonic cartilage cell cultures, it was shown that a particular fraction of an aqueous extract of the whole embryo was necessary for the establishment of cultures of cartilage — producing cells and that another embryo extract fraction would inhibit their establishment. It remains true, however, that many long established cell lines are clearly aberrant in at least chromosome composition, and that cell death may, in fact, be a normal programmed event. Thus studies of the differentiation of cells in culture represent studies of a model of the natural situation and not the natural situation itself.

The technical advantages of using cell cultures are immense. Such cultures allow, at least in principle, all the techniques of microbiology to be applied to mammalian cells and have the advantage over systems like the cellular slime mould of enabling the coupling between growth and cell differentiation to be investigated as well as being, of course, a much closer model to the embryonic cell. In some cases it has been possible to obtain systems remarkably analogous to the β-galactosidase induction in *E. coli* K12 as well.

Tomkins and his co-workers have shown that in a rat cell line derived from a hepatoma (i.e. liver tumour) the synthesis of the enzyme tyrosine transaminase is dependent on the addition and continued presence of corticosteroids which act as inducers for the enzyme. However, there appear to be fundamental differences between the way in which the lac operon inducers act, and the way in which corticosteroids act on liver cells. Tomkins [33] has suggested that the corticosteroids act, not at the transcriptional level by controlling the activity of the structural gene (Fig. 3.16, GS), but at the translational level by controlling the stability of the mRNA.

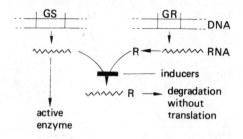

Fig. **3.16** Control of tyrosine transaminase synthesis in liver cells. R = repressor protein. Redrawn from [33].

The cell, it is suggested, continuously synthesises mRNA molecules for tyrosine transaminase and a protein repressor molecule (Fig. 3.16, R). In the absence of inducer the repressor molecules combine with the tyrosine transaminase mRNA preventing its translation and stimulating its degradation. Inducer molecules prevent this combination of mRNA with repressors and cause the dissociation of mRNA-repressor complexes already formed. The mRNA is now free to be translated into tyrosine transaminase on polysomes in the cytoplasm. This theory is based largely on an analysis of the effect of actinomycin D on enzyme induction. Actinomycin D has a number of 'paradoxical' effects in this system causing 'superinduction' in the presence of inducers and delaying the reduction of the rate of enzyme synthesis which normally follows inducer removal. These effects are explicable in terms of the model of Fig. 3.16 because repressor (R) synthesis is also actinomycin D sensitive, and it is assumed that there is a significant pool of mRNA-repressor complexes. Dissociation of these complexes liberates mRNA thus causing the 'paradoxical' effects of actinomycin D. (compare p. 26).

It is a weakness of this theory that so much of it rests, directly or indirectly, on studies of the effects of actinomycin D. It is difficult to be sure that an inhibitory drug does not have side effects that are unsuspected, and which vitiate conclusions drawn from its use. Actinomycin D is a lipophilic compound and thus will bind strongly to membranes. Conclusions drawn from its use have to be treated with caution, therefore, and it has been suggested that many of Tomkins's observations could be explained by a differential effect of actinomycin D on the degradation (as opposed to the synthesis) of tyrosine transaminase [34].

The hepatoma cells used by Tomkins can be grown in synchronous culture and studies of the induction of tyrosine transaminase at different periods of the cell cycle (Fig. 3.10) have shown that induction can only occur if corticosteroids are added during the late G1 and S phases. There seems to be inhibition of transcription of both GS and GR (Fig. 3.16) during G2, mitosis and early G1 since preinduced cells can continue to synthesise enzyme during these periods.

One way in which these regulatory mechanisms might be established unambiguously would be to isolate and characterise the appropriate mutants. Unfortunately it is difficult to devise suitable selective pressures for such mutants (which must be expected to be rare) in tissue culture media owing to its complex composition. A further difficulty is that even if it were possible to obtain the desired regulatory mutants it is not yet possible to analyse them genetically. Tissue cells do not normally need to possess any system of genetic recombination, in fact such a system might well prove disastrous to the whole organism, and so it is not likely that any mating system will be found amongst tissue culture cells. Recently, however, this difficulty has been circumvented by the discovery that multinucleate cells may be constructed by cell fusion induced by virus particles. The Sendai virus (which causes an influenza type of disease and which was first isolated in Japan) has proved particularly useful in these studies. Virus particles are inactivated with u.v. light (to render them non-lethal) and incubated with tissue culture cells when they promote random fusions giving rise to multinucleate cells. The fate of these heterokaryons depends critically on the nature of the cells from which they were derived. In favourable circumstances it is possible to obtain hybrid cell lines from such heterokaryons containing chromosomes or chromosome material from more than one nucleus in the now uninucleate cells. The resulting hybrid cells will be genetically recombinant if they were formed from cells containing different genotypes. In this way it has been possible to localise a number of genes to particular chromosomes, and as techniques improve the precision and scope of these procedures may rival those of bacterial genetics.

Direct use of the cell fusion techniques for the study of cell differentiation in tissue culture cells has been hampered by the, not unreasonable, fact that when two differentiated cells are fused together their differentiated functions (particularly if these should involve an elaborate system of cytoplasmic organelles) are usually lost rapidly from the heterokaryon. However, recently, part of some differentiated functions has been preserved amongst the hybrid products from cell fusions [35] and so there seems to be no inherent reason why these techniques should not prove as useful to the study of differentiation as have been the studies of bacterial genetics to studies of the control of β-galactosidase synthesis in *E. coli*.

Studies of tissue culture cells represent attempts to combine the technical advantage of microbial systems with the complexity of the cell differentiations seen in multicellular organisms. Such attempts have not proved very successful but they have shown that:

(1) in some instances posttranscriptional

29

controls are of key importance, and
(2) that genetic analysis is possible in tissue culture cells.

3.7 Metamorphosis.

The conversion of a tadpole to a frog or a caterpillar to a butterfly is, in many respects, closely analogous to embryological development. In these organisms it is as if the normal embryological development has been divided into two phases by the insertion of a prolonged and freeliving larval stage. If this analogy is correct, of course, then studies of the control of metamorphosis should also reveal the way in which embryogenesis is regulated and, from the practical point of view, it is usually much easier to work with larvae than it is with embryos.

The metamorphoses undergone by insects and amphibians have a number of similarities. Both sets of processes are initiated and dependent on hormones (ecdysone in insects, thyroid hormones in amphibia) and may be distinguished from purely adaptational processes by the fact that they are begun and often completed *in anticipation* of a change in the environment. Metamorphosis thus represents the triggering off, by hormonal signals, of a programme of differentiation in cells already determined in the embryological sense. Thus, there is an unusually clear cut distinction here between the time at which determination occurs and the time at which differentiation occurs. Hadorn [36] has exploited this to investigate the stability and nature of determination itself in *Drosophila*. Here the cells which are to form the adult structures are present in the larvae in the form of groups of cells with no apparent function in the larval stage — the imaginal discs. Several sets of discs are distributed about the larval body and during pupation the cells of the disc give rise to the adult structures at the same time as the larval structures are undergoing destruction.

In the amphibia, too, there is seen the simultaneous destruction of larval structures and development of adult tissues. The most dramatic example of this kind of programmed destruction of a tissue is the resorption of tadpole tail. This process is known to be dependent on the prior induction of new degradative enzymes which in turn implies the selective activation of genes whose function is to destroy the cell. The importance of loss of function and structure cannot be over emphasised in all differentiating systems.

The transition from an aquatic to a partially terrestrial mode of life involves the metamorphosing tadpole in a drastic reorganisation of its nitrogen metabolism. In particular the enzymes of the urea cycle have to be synthesised *de novo* by the liver cells. This process is known [37] to be induced by the thyroid hormones and to involve the synthesis not only of ribosomal and other RNA molecules but also of phospholipid and other membrane components. The connection, in this instance, of protein and membrane synthesis is particularily close and striking. Just prior to the appearance of urea cycle enzymes in the liver cell there is a massive synthesis of new ribosomes which appear to be very strongly bound to endoplasmic reticulum membranes. Since there is also a massive turnover of phospholipid material at the same time, it seems likely that these new ribosomes become associated with the new membranes. Electron microscope studies of thin sections of cells, at this stage, confirm that there is a shift of ribosomes from simple vesicular structures to a more complex system of double lamellae which first appear in the perinuclear region. That the changes in RNA and phospholipid metabolism do, in fact, represent the topographical segregation of polysomes on new membranes, is strongly supported by the observation that also associated with these new membrane structures are a class of mitochondria with poorly developed cristae and which, histological studies have suggested, contain the urea cycle enzyme carbamyl phosphate synthase.

These studies on metamorphosis in insects and amphibia thus represent the most complex, and complete, model system imaginable for studies of cell differentiation in embryogenesis. In particular such studies:

(1) offer the clearest instance yet known in which determination and differentiation can be disentangled

(2) emphasise the key role played by hormonal control mechanisms, and

(3) they offer the clearest example so far studied of the interrelationship of molecular/biochemical events and cytological changes.

References

[1] Brenner, S., Jacob, F. and Meselson, M. (1961), *Nature*, **190**, 576–580.

[2] Wood, W. B. and Berg, P. (1962), *Proc. Nat. Acad. Sci.* (US), **48**, 94–104.

[3] Burgess, R. P., Travers, A. A., Dunn, J. J. and Bautz, E. K. F. (1969), *Nature*, **221**, 43–47.

[4] Bautz, E. K. F., Bautz, F. A. and Dunn, J. J. (1970), *Nature*, **223**, 1022–1024.

[5] Travers, A. A. (1971), *Nature*, **229**, 69–71.

[6] Cohen, S. S. (1968), *Virus Induced Enzymes*, Columbia University Press, New York.

[7] Levine, M. (1969), *Ann. Rev. Gen.*, **3**, 323–342.

[8] Beckwith, J. and Zipser, D. (1970), *The Lac Operon*, Cold Spring Harbour Laboratory, New York.

[9] Jacob, F. and Monod, J. (1961), *J. Mol. Biol.*, **3**, 318–356.

[10] Woods, R.A. (1973), *Biochemical Genetics*, Chapman and Hall, London.

[11] Lewin, B. M. (1970), *The Molecular Basis of Gene Expression*, J. Wiley and Son, London.

[12] Monod, J. and Jacob, F. (1961), *Cold Spring Harbour Symp.*, **26**, 389–401.

[13] Mitchison, J. M. (1971), *The Biology of the Cell Cycle*, Cambridge University Press, Cambridge.

[14] Losick, R. and Sonenshein, A. L. (1969), *Nature*, **224**, 35–37.

[15] Sadoff, H. L., Celikol, E. and Engelbreckt, H. L. (1970), *Proc. Nat. Acad. Sci.* (US), **66**, 844–849.

[16] Mandelstam, J. (1971), *Symp. Soc. Exp. Biol.*, **25**, 1–26.

[17] Szjulmajster, J. (1973), *Symp. Soc. gen. Microbiol.*, **23**, 45–83.

[18] Novikoff, A. B. and Holtzman, E. (1971), *Cells and Organelles*, Holt, Reinhard and Winston, New York.

[19] Davis, M. (1973), *Functions of Biological Membranes*, Chapman and Hall, London.

[20] See articles by Carr, N. G., Dworkin, M. and Hopwood, D. A. (1973), *Symp. Soc. gen. Microbiol.*, **23**.

[21] Ohno, S. (1970), *Evolution by Gene Duplication*, Allen and Unwin, London.

[22] Southern, E. M. (1970), *Nature*, **227**, 794–798.

[23] Gall, J. G. and Pardue, M. L. (1970), *Science*, **168**, 1356–1358.

[24] Britten, R. J. and Kohne, D. E. (1968), *Science*, **161**, 529–540.

[25] Garrod, D.J. and Ashworth J.M. (1973), *Symp. Soc. gen. Microbiol.*, **23**, 407–427.

[26] Quance, J. and Ashworth, J. M. (1972), *Biochem. J.*, **126**, 609–615.

[27] Bonner, J. T. (1972), *Ann. Rev. Microbiol.*, **25**, 75–92.

[28] Bonner, J. T. (1972), *Proc. Nat. Acad. Sci.* (US), **65**, 110–113.

[29] Wright, B. E. (1966), *Science*, **153**, 830–837.

[30] Moore, G. E. and McLimans, W. F. (1968), *J. Theoret. Biol.*, **20**, 217–226.

[31] Konigsberg, I. R. (1963), *Science*, **140**, 1273–1284.

[32] Coon, H. G. (1966), *Proc. Nat. Acad. Sci.* (US), **55**, 66–73.

[33] Tomkins, G. M., Gelehrter, T. D., Martin, D., Samuels, H. H. and Thompson, E. B. (1966), *Science*, **166**, 1474–1480.

[34] Reel, J. R. and Kenney, F. T. (1968), *Proc. Nat. Acad. Sci.* (US), **61**, 200–206.

[35] Harris, H. (1969), *Cell Fusion*, Oxford University Press, Oxford.

[36] Hadorn, E. (1967), In *Major Problems in Developmental Biology*, Academic Press: New York, pp. 85–104.

[37] Tata, J. R. (1971), *Symp. Soc. Exp. Biol.*, **25**, 163–182.

4 Special systems, the classical approach

In the preceding sections it has been assumed, more or less explicitly, that cell differentiation is fundamentally a problem of differential gene activity i.e. different genes are active in different cell types but all cells have the same genetic information. In model systems such as the phage, sporulation and spore germination, where there is only one cell involved, the problem must clearly be one of time dependent changes in gene activity, but in multicellular, and especially embryonic systems, this is not so obvious. Indeed Weismann in the 19th century suggested that the origin of differences between embryonic cells had to do with differences in what he termed their 'nucleoplasm'. The simplest hypothesis, he suggested, 'would be to suppose that at each division of the nucleus, its specific substance divides into two halves of unequal quality, so that the cell-bodies would also be transformed . . . ' Of course such an ordered parcelling out of genes amongst the cells of the embryo must leave the germ cells unaffected and so Weismann's theory also necessitated a qualitative distinction between the somatic and the germ cells. This theory did not survive long in its original form, but it can claim to be one of the most important of all embryological theories since it stimulated much of the classical work in embryology and in a sense it still survives, albeit in a much altered and sophisticated form, in the 'master-slave' hypothesis of Callan (see Section 4.1.1). Barth [1] has lucidly described the attempts to prove or disprove Weismann's theory and

discusses the transplantation experiments which are now taken to prove that fully differentiated cells contain a full complement of genes. These experiments utilise the fact that amphibian eggs are so large that nuclei and other materials can be readily injected into the cytoplasm and the developmental consequences of such treatments studied. The most convincing of these experiments was done by Gurdon who showed that a diploid nucleus taken from an intestinal cell of the African clawed toad, *Xenopus laevis* could, when injected into a *Xenopus* egg whose nucleus had been inactivated, stimulate normal development of the egg and eventually lead to the production of fully mature and fertile frogs. This experiment implies that differentiated cells have a complete set of genes but, unfortunately, similar experiments to Gurdon's carried out earlier by Briggs and King with the frog *Rana*, have given rather different results. It is thus not possible to say that permanent and irreversible modification of what Weismann termed the nucleoplasm never occurs. Indeed, despite the fact that careful measurements of the DNA content of the diploid nuclei of cells have shown that the cells of most tissues of the adult have the same DNA content; cases are known (see Section 4.1.2) where this is not so. However, at the present time it seems more useful to regard such cases, and the Briggs and King experiments, as the exceptions that prove the rule that all cells of an organism have an identical genetic complement and that they, therefore, differ in

33

the activity and not the nature of their genes. This conclusion is supported by careful genetic analysis of developmental mutants in higher organisms.

Many lethal developmental mutants in higher organisms cause death in a highly specific and reproducible fashion at a definite time in development. Typically, development proceeds normally up to a certain point and then characteristic aberrant structures are produced and death ensues. Thus mice, homozygous for the brachyrury gene, develop normally up to the 10–11th day of development when they die as a result of aberrant notocord (skeletal) differentiation. The implication of numerous observations of this sort is that development proceeds normally in the mutant prior to the 10th day because the brachyrury gene is inactive up to that time. At the 10th day the notocord cells activate the gene, get a mutant gene product and consequently fail to form a normal skeleton. It is significant that in this, as in many other such cases, other cells remain unaffected until engulfed by a general necrosis and thus the brachyrury gene acts not only at a specific time in development, but also only in certain cells i.e. its activation is both time and tissue-specific. Even in those cases where the mutant appears to be affected in numerous tissues simultaneously (pleiotropic mutations), it is often possible to show that many of these complications are due to secondary effects of a mutation whose primary effect is tissue specific. Thus dwarfism in mice gives rise to individuals about 1/3 the size of normal mice, and having numerous metabolic defects and abnormalities. The metabolic defects are due to abnormalities in a number of endocrine organs and these, in turn, are due to a primary defect in the eosinophilic cells of the anterior lobe of the pituitary gland which produce growth hormone.

In some cases it has been possible to show that the tissue specificity of gene action is a result of the tissue specific production of a protein. The clearest example of this is the characteristic change in isoenzyme patterns from tissue to tissue (Section 4.5). In this case there can be no doubt that different genes are active to different extents in different tissues, and in the same tissue at different stages of development. Study of the isoenzyme patterns of lactate dehydrogenase in in-bred strains of mice have also revealed a fascinating case of the tissue specificity of expression of a regulatory gene. Wild type mice have B-type subunits in the lactate dehydrogenase of their erythrocytes (and many other tissues). However, mice homozygous for the Ldr-1 gene have no B-subunits in their erythrocyte lactate dehydrogenase although the isoenzyme pattern of all other tissues is the same in the mutant as in the wild type. Thus the ability to synthesise B-subunits is present in the Ldr-1 mutants, what has been affected is a regulatory gene which is only active in the erythrocytes. Other detailed studies of in-bred mouse strains (reviewed in 2) have revealed other instances of the tissue specific expression of both structural and regulatory genes.

Genetics plays a role in Biology analogous to that played by Thermodynamics in the Physical Sciences. Its observations and arguments are internally self-consistent and quite independent of any theories of the nature of the gene, mutation etc., and provide a set of observations with which any mechanistic theory must be compatible. Thus the genetic evidence for the notion of differential gene activity, which stems largely from studies of in-bred laboratory strains of mice and rats, coupled with the transplantation experiments of Gurdon justify the present concentration of effort on attempts to understand how genes can be activated (and repressed) at specific times in specific cells of the developing embryo.

Work with model systems (Chapter 3) has suggested that such controls might be sought at the level of transcription, translation, at the point of degradation of macromolecular components, and also, of course, at the level of the structure and activity of the macromolecular components themselves. We have seen how the unusually large size of the egg and the largely fortuitous establishment of in-bred strains of rats and mice have helped establish the notion of differential gene activity, we now have to see if there are other highly specialised systems in which we can study these other processes.

4.1 Chromosome structure and function

The DNA of eukaryote cells is organised into organelles — the chromosomes — which contain in addition to DNA, basic proteins (histones), acidic proteins and RNA. The ratio of DNA : RNA : protein varies from tissue to tissue, but 'typical' values are those for rat liver — $1\cdot00$ DNA: $1\cdot00$ histone: $0\cdot67$ acidic protein: $0\cdot043$ RNA.

During most of the cell cycle the chromosomes are, in all except a few special cells, invisible, and when they do become visible, at division, they appear to be condensed and not active in transcription. It is therefore difficult to determine the part played by the various chromosomal components in determining the structure and regulating the activity of the DNA molecules. Much of what is known about chromosome structure and function has come from a study of the extraordinary chromosomes of the oocytes of amphibia, and the salivary glands of fly larvae.

4.1.1 Lampbrush chromosomes

Lampbrush chromosomes are found in the cells (oocytes) which will eventually become the eggs of a wide variety of organisms. They appear as hairy threads, (Fig. 4.1) which develop in the oocyte from normal pachytene chromosomes, last for several months or years whilst the oocyte matures, and finally contract to form normal meiotic bivalents prior to the last stages of meiosis and formation of the egg. Lampbrush chromosomes are thus in the diplotene stage of meiosis. The chromonema consists of two double helices of DNA and the chromomeres (so called because they stain strongly with DNA specific stains) represent regions along the chromosome in which supercoiling of the DNA occurs. A loop consists of one DNA double helix with associated RNA and protein. The loops are always paired and each loop has a characteristic, genetically determined structure. The loops are visible without staining procedures because of the matrix of protein which they contain. One end of the loop appears to have more matrix than the other. When actinomycin D is added to oocytes the matrix is stripped from the loop and the naked DNA fibril collapses onto the chromomere. If the drug is now washed out and a pulse of radioactive uridine is given, the label appears first at the end of the loop where the matrix was thinnest and then spreads over the loop as it reforms, suggesting that the DNA is being 'spun out' from one side of the chromomere, is actively synthesising RNA and acquiring a protein coat as it traverses the region of the loop and is finally 'wound in' at the other side of the chromomere. Examination of carefully spread lampbrush chromosomes in the electron microscope has confirmed this interpretation and shows the matrix to have a structure similar to that seen in the nucleolus (Fig. 4.6 p. 45) where it is known that ribosomal RNA synthesis is occurring.

The chromomere thus contains DNA (and its associated proteins) in a supercoiled, condensed and inactive state whereas the loops contain DNA in an uncoiled, diffuse and active conformation.

The total amount of DNA in a chromomere and its pair of loops, is about the same as in the entire genome of $E. coil$ ($\sim 10^{-14}$g), and yet each loop pair acts as if it were a functional unit for RNA (and thus protein) synthesis. Since the average protein would need very much less than this amount of DNA to specify its primary structure, it is clear that if each loop does indeed correspond to one gene — and loop patterns are inherited as if they were Mendelian alleles — then there is very much more DNA in the loop, and active in RNA synthesis, than might be expected. To account for this Callan suggested [3] that there were many copies of a structural gene present in each loop. This is difficult to reconcile with the genetic evidence that only one allele seems to be borne on each chromosome, and also with the single hit kinetics of mutagenesis. To meet these objections Callan assumed that not all copies of the gene were equivalent. One copy — the master gene — was unique in that it, and it alone, participated in genetic recombination and represented the Mendelian allele. All the other copies of the gene — the slaves — had to undergo a process of restitution whereby they checked their base sequences against that of the master gene before they became available for transcription. In this way mutations in the master gene can be transmitted to the slave *genes* and thus produce altered proteins but, should mutations arise in the slave genes, they are eliminated during the restitution process. A distinction is thus made between genes as transmitters of genetic information, and genes as templates for transcription. Thus Callan's hypothesis suggests that a chromomere and loop represent one family of genes. The loop contains those slaves actually serving as templates for RNA synthesis, whilst the master is in that part of the chromomere where the matrix is thinnest, checking the base sequences of the slaves before they enter the loop and begin the journey from one side of the chromomere to the other. This stimulating theory has not yet been proved correct but it accounts for many of the observation of the behaviour of lampbrush chromosomes and can be reconciled with much of the genetics of higher organisms. However, this theory would

predict that most genes would be present in many copies (reiterated) in the genome. Reiterated copies of sequences are known to occur in eukaryote DNA (see p. 21) but most of the DNA is present as single copies. It could be argued that whilst every cell has a copy of all master genes, it only makes slave copies of those masters it is actually going to use (gene amplification). This appears to be true of the ribosomal genes in oocytes (see Section 4.2) but the constancy of the DNA content of different cells argues against it being generally true. Thomas has summarised the evidence in favour of the Callan hypothesis [4] and these ideas have been reviewed in [5].

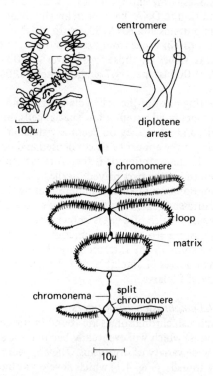

Fig. 4.1 Structure of lampbrush chromosomes from the newt (*Triturus viridescens*) Redrawn from [4]

36

The oocyte may remain in the arrested diplotene state with its chromosomes in the lampbrush configuration for months or years. During this time it is continuously synthesising RNA, and calculations suggest that the RNA synthesised can be accounted for by the enormous amount of mRNA present in the mature egg. It thus seems that the lampbrush configuration is forced on the chromosome by the sheer necessity of synthesising an inordinate amount of cytoplasm to form an egg, and to provide that egg with a store of mRNA (in an inactive state, see p. 48) for utilisation during the early cleavage stages of embryogenesis.

There are at least two other ways in which the chromosome configuration can change to meet similar imbalances in volume between nucleus and cytoplasm. One of these is also found in oocytes and will be discussed in Section 4.2, the other is found in the salivary glands of fly larvae.

4.1.2 Polytene chromosomes.

Normally, just prior to cell division, mitosis leads to the orderly separation of the daughter chromosomes and the formation of two separate nuclei. In the differentiation of salivary glands of the larvae of a number of flies, however, this procedure breaks down; there is no mitosis and the daughter chromosomes do not separate but remain stuck together. The DNA/cytoplasm ratio is maintained by the growth of the cytoplasm and so the net result is the production of enormous cells containing, in the case of Drosophila, some 500–1000 copies of each chromatid, and in the case of the gnat Chironomous about $4-8 \times 10^3$ such copies. These multiple copies of the chromatids remain joined by their chromomeres, and the precise alignment of numerous chromomeres give rise to the characteristic banded structure of these polytene (many stranded) chromosomes. They measure about 1mm in length and can be some 50μm wide which makes them visible to the naked eye. The work of classical geneticists has correlated alterations in particular bands with particular mutations and it is possible that each band corresponds to one Mendelian gene. Thus the band structure of the polytene chromosome of the salivary gland is identical to the band structure of the polytene chromosomes of the foot pad, or the malphighian tubules, or indeed to any of the cells which contain polytene chromosomes. Careful observations of the band pattern in the same tissue at different times of development, or in different tissues at the same time of development, reveal slight irregularities in pattern, however, due to a general loosening of the chromosomal structure. These looser bands are called 'puffs' and studies with radioactive RNA precursors have shown that RNA synthesis proceeds most rapidly at the puffed regions. A survey of puffing patterns has shown that they are highly specific and changes are, indeed, time and tissue-specific, as would be expected if puffing indicates gene activation.

In one case the appearance of a specific polypeptide has been correlated with the formation of a specific puff. The larvae of two different species of Chironomous have salivary gland secretions which differ in composition. C.tentans has no granules in certain of its salivary gland cells, and its mucopolysaccharide secretory product lacks a polypeptide present in that from C.pallidivittatus, which characteristically does have an array of granules in certain of its salivary gland cells. Crosses between the two species have shown that the ability to form these granules and the complete secretory product is inherited as a typical Mendelian character, and is carried by a gene on chromosome 4 near the centromere. At this point on the C.pallidivittatus salivary gland chromosome there is a prominent puff which is absent from the homologous chromosome of C.tentans. The correlation between the appearance on chromosome 4 of a specific puff, and the appearance in some of the salivary gland cells of the granules,

37

and the appearance in the mucopolysaccharide secretion product of a specific polypeptide, is perfect [6, 7]. Careful microanalysis of the RNA in separated salivary gland chromosomes of *C. tentans* has shown that RNA molecules of different base composition are synthesised at different puffs, and so the evidence for the belief that a puff represents a gene actively transcribing seems overwhelming. So, just as a loop in a lampbrush chromosome represents the DNA of the chromomere in a diffuse, active configuration, so a puff represents the DNA of a chromosomal band (formed by the precise alignment of homologous chromomeres) in a diffuse, active conformation.

Differentiation in insects is controlled by hormones (Section 3.7) and an elegant confirmation of the idea that puffs represent activated genes, has been the work of Clever and others who have shown that when the hormone ecdysone is injected into the larvae of *Chironomous*, thus causing premature pupation, a certain specific set of puffs on the salivary chromosomes appear prematurely in a specific, time dependent sequence. Associated with this is an alteration, in the nature of the secretion, of salivary glands which is now used to form the pupation shell instead of the larval feeding net. The prematurely induced sequence of puffs is identical with that sequence observed during normal pupation, and the specificity of action of ecdysone is shown by the fact that in different species it has quite different, but always highly characteristic, effects. In *Acrocotopus* the primary effect of ecdysone is the condensation and disappearance of puffs, and in *Drosophila* about 30 puffs appear simultaneously rather than in sequence. The mechanism whereby ecdysone acts is uncertain, it may act directly on a puff or indirectly by causing alterations in the salt balance of the nucleus. Whatever the mechanism might be, the effect of ecdysone is not only species-specific but also tissue-specific — the ecdysone induced puffs of

the salivary gland chromosomes are not the same as those of the foot pad — as would be expected for an agent which caused differential gene activation.

Microspectrophotometric analysis of the DNA content of the bands in polytene chromosomes has shown that each has an amount of DNA comparable to the entire genome of *E. coli* and so, as in the case of the chromomeres and loops of the lampbrush chromosome, there appears to be many copies of each gene in one band. This conclusion is reinforced by studies of the DNA contents of homologous bands in the two closely related sub-species of *Chironomous, C. thummi thummi* and *C. thummi piger*. In these organisms the band structure of the chromosomes is qualitatively very similar but some bands in *C. thummi thummi* are thicker and larger than the homologous ones in *C. thummi piger*. These thicker bands have been shown to contain exactly 2^n times the DNA of the bands of the other sub-species (the value of n varies from one band to another). Thus a band is not only equivalent to a Mendelian allele and a unit of structure and function but also, it appears, a unit of replication as well. The further implication is that independent controls exist which regulate the degree of amplification of each gene. These controls might be tissue specific, and in one specific case — the ribosomal genes — it has been possible to show that such tissue specific controls do exist (see Section 4.2). However, in general puffs do not contain more DNA than the band from which they are formed — they are sites of RNA synthesis not of DNA synthesis. The exception which proves this rule are the *Sciarid* flies where particular puffs have been shown to be sites of specific DNA synthesis and thus gene amplification. No other example of DNA puffs have been reported but, of course, such puffs would have to be massive before they would be visible cytologically and a small degree of specific amplification might

38

well occur unobserved.

Studies of the DNA-DNA hybridization kinetics of DNA from *Drosophila* salivary glands, has suggested that, contrary to the cytological data, most of a band in a salivary gland chromosome consists of single copies of unique sequences. The occurrence of conflicting evidence of this kind usually signifies a fundamental defect in our understanding of phenomena but at the moment it is hard to see where that deficiency lies [5].

4.1.3. Heterochromatin

The chromosomes of normal cells not undergoing division are in a relatively uncoiled state, this uncoiling is maximal in those regions of the chromosome which do not stain very intensely (euchromatin), and is minimal in those regions of the chromosome which do stain intensely (heterochromatin). Some nuclei show a stable non-random pattern of heterochromatisation of their chromosomes. The clearest example is seen in some cells from female mammals. Cells of female mammals usually contain two X chromosomes whereas cells of male mammals contain one X and one Y chromosome. However, rarely organisms with only one X chromosome are produced (XO) and these have a female phenotype so only one active X is needed to produce a female. The Y chromosome contains few if any genes (apart from the sex determinants), but the X chromosome contains a number. Analyses of the expression of these (particularily useful have been a number of X-linked coat colour genes in mice) have suggested that in the process of differentiation in female mammals there is a random inactivation of one of the two X chromosomes. This suggestion is supported by the finding that it is possible to obtain clones of skin cells from females heterozygous for glucose-6-phosphate dehydrogenase (an X-linked gene) which have either one but never both of the allellic forms of glucose-6-phosphate dehydrogenase. At least one other similar case is known — the gene for hyperuricemia — and although this does not prove that the whole of one X chromosome is inactivated to give two populations of cells in the skin of female mammals it strongly suggest it. Barr noticed that in many female cells (but never in male cells) a late replicating, heterochromatic body called the 'Barr body' was present in the nucleus. It seems likely that the Barr body represents the inactivated X-chromosome and thus this represents another instance where it is possible to correlate the condensed, supercoiled state of a chromosome with biochemical inactivity. It seems likely that the diffuse, euchromatic and the condensed, heterochromatic states represent two possible conformations which any chromosome, or any part of any chromosome, may adopt, and that there is is a close similarity between on the one hand the euchromatic, puffed and loop regions of normal, polytene and lampbrush chromosomes, and on the other, the heterochromatic, banded and chromomeric portions of those same chromosomes.

Other staining procedures have been used (particularily fluorescent stains) to demonstrate differential staining of parts of chromosomes. These differences are almost certainly due to differences in the supercoiled structure of parts of chromosomes just as are the differences between euchromatin and heterochromatin.

Recently, RNA labelling has been observed in isolated polytene chromosomes exposed to radioactive precursors, indicating that the chromosome itself contains the entire biosynthetic machinery needed for RNA synthesis. The exact nature of this machinery and the way in which it is controlled cannot be determined from purely cytological studies, however.

4.1.4. Biochemical studies

Unfortunately, biochemical studies of chromosome function have not yet reached the stage where the behaviour of lampbrush chromosomes and the control of puffing and heterochromatisation can be interpreted in molecular terms. Associated with the DNA in the chromosome are two kinds of protein—the histones and the acidic proteins—and RNA molecules. Somehow these molecules must regulate the activity of the DNA.

The histones comprise a rather homogenous family of relatively low molecular weight proteins, all of which are basic. Five main types have been recognised which differ particularly in their basicity and in their arginine and lysine contents. The dye eosin appears to bind preferentially to the lysine rich families of histone, and the dye fast green to the arginine-rich families. Nuclei in a variety of tissues do not stain equally with these two reagents and even within a single nucleus different chromosomes may stain differently. During the differentiation of a cell the staining properties of the chromosome may also change, for example the nucleus of the prospective red blood cell becomes progressively more eosinophilic as differentiation proceeds. However, it is most unlikely that the histones themselves determine whether a gene is active in transcription or not. Puffed and unpuffed regions of polytene chromosomes stain equally intensively with histochemical reagents for histones, although treatment with non-specific protein stains, show that puffs have a higher protein content than do unpuffed regions. This extra protein must therefore be acidic rather than basic. It is also difficult to see how histones could regulate gene activity since there are so few different molecular species and since it has become clear that the histones of widely different organisms are astonishingly similar. Histone IV of pea plants and calf thymus has been purified and the amino acid sequence of both proteins determined. There are hardly any differences which implies that there has been no change in the structure (and thus the function) of this protein since cows and peas last had a common ancestor eons ago. This implies that histones play so crucial a role that virtually any change in their structure is lethal and, by the same token, they are thus unlikely to be directly involved in regulating gene activity since this obviously has been subject to considerable evolutionary change.

Chromosomal RNA consists of a polydisperse high molecular weight fraction which probably consists of molecules caught in the act of being transcribed when the chromosome was isolated and a very low molecular weight fraction which, it has been claimed [8], comprise a specific class of molecules characterized by a high dihydropyrimidine content. However, dihydropyrimidine is also characteristic of transfer RNA and the wide variations in the amount of this species of RNA, which chromosomes contain when isolated by different techniques, suggests that it may represent degraded fragments of transfer RNA which have become adsorbed onto the chromosomes in the course of their preparation.

The acidic proteins found in chromosomes comprise a very heterogenous set of high molecular weight proteins. Study of these proteins has been hampered by the fact that they are insoluble and tend to aggregate in solutions of low ionic strength. Thus, although it has been claimed that there are marked differences in the nature of the chromosome-bound, acidic protein fractions from a number of tissues, of the same organism and in the same tissue at different times of development (as would be expected if these molecules were indeed involved in regulating gene activity) the drastic extraction methods used might well mean that these differences are artefactual.

Support for the idea that it is the acidic proteins which provide the specificity of gene regulation rather than the histones has, however, come from studies of the effect of these proteins on transcription *in vitro*. Mammalian transcriptases have not yet been obtained in an homogeous state but purified mammalian DNA is an acceptable template for the bacterial enzyme (Table 1, p. 11). Under the usual assay conditions, however, only sequences present in a concentration of at least 10^3 copies/genome will be transcribed. Addition of histones to these DNA preparations causes a marked decrease in the rate of RNA synthesised but, since DNA-histone complexes are insoluble in the dilute salt solutions which have to be used for the enzyme assays, such an inhibition is not convincing evidence for a physiological role of histones in 'masking' parts of the DNA. It is not sufficient to show that an agent reduces the rate or amount of RNA synthesised; what is needed to explain the differential gene activation seen during differentiation is a *specific* inhibition of the synthesis of some RNA molecules but not others.

Paul and Gilmour [9] have used DNA: RNA hybridization to determine the nature of the RNA molecules synthesized using various templates and thus investigate the specificity of RNA synthesis. DNA and native chromatin were used as templates and the RNA molecules so produced used in hybridization experiments with purified DNA. The RNA sample, prepared from chromatin templates, hybridized with a much smaller fraction of the DNA than did that obtained from the DNA template, showing that transcription is restricted in native chromatin to certain regions of the DNA. Comparison of the RNA, produced *in vitro* from chromatin templates, with pulse labelled RNA produced *in vivo* from the appropriate tissue showed that the RNA synthesized *in vitro* was similar to that made *in vivo* and thus the restrictions seen on transcription of chromatin were of physiological significance. Competition hybridization experiments showed that the RNA made *in vitro* from different chromatins prepared from different tissues were themselves different (Fig. 4.2).

When purified DNA was mixed with histones and acidic proteins in the presence of high salt

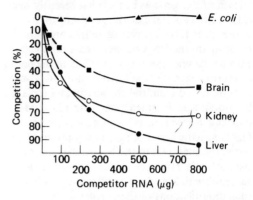

Fig. 4.2. Radioactive RNA from liver chromatin was hybridised to DNA in the presence of RNA prepared from brain, kidney, *E. coli* and liver and the amount by which these preparations diminished the binding of the radioactive RNA to the DNA (% competition) was measured. Redrawn from [9].

concentrations and then dialysed to remove the salts, a chromatin preparation was obtained which had similar properties to the native material — showing that chromatin complexes can spontaneously reassemble. It is now possible to attempt to reconstitute the chromatin preparation in stages by adding first one component, and then the others and see, at each stage, which component confers the specific restriction of transcription. Unfortunately these experiments have not given clear cut results since there appears, not perhaps unexpectedly, to be synergistic effects between the various protein components, but the acidic protein fraction seem to provide much of the specificity. In agreement with this is the observation that if chromatins are reconstituted from DNA, histones and non-histone proteins obtained from different tissues, then the transcription products are those appropriate to the tissue which provide the non-histone proteins.

The key question is how do histones and the acidic proteins act in molecular terms? Little is known of this process but use has recently been made of the special case of spermatogenesis in the trout [10] to investigate this problem. In trout sperm the DNA molecules are complexed with protamines not histones. Thus in the course of spermatogenesis, the histone molecules have to be removed from the chromatin and replaced by protamines. In at least one case a histone molecule is removed as a consequence of a highly specific series of phosphorylations at serine residues near to the N-terminal end of the molecule. Histones are also known to be susceptible to acetylation and it is possible that such modifications of their structure (perhaps catalysed or controlled by the non-histone proteins of chromatin) could lead to the tissue specific masking of stretches of the DNA. Recently it has been shown that the enzyme which catalyses the phosphorylation of histones is activated by cyclic-AMP [11] which is a well characterized mediator of a number of hormone induced processes. It is not known if cyclic-AMP is involved in spermatogenesis, but it is clear that studies of this kind of process are likely to lead to an understanding of the forces which can lead to a dissociation of histones from DNA.

It is clear that the special problems faced by gametes have led to these cells exhibiting in an exaggerated form, processes which are probably quite general. In particular these studies have established that:

(1) the chromomeres are units of structure, replication and function and

(2) that each chromomere contains far more DNA than is needed to code for the amino acid sequence of one protein molecule

(3) the same region of the chromosome may adopt one of perhaps several different conformations depending on whether it is being replicated, transcribed or is inactive.

(4) different conformations of the chromosome can be recognized by characteristic alterations in its staining properties

(5) heterochromatic regions of normal chromosomes represent inactive regions and appear to be equivalent ot the chromomeres of lampbrush chromosomes and the bands of polytene chromosomes, whereas the euchromatic regions of normal chromosomes represent active regions of chromosomes and are equivalent to the loops of lampbrush chromosomes and the puffs of polytene chromosomes.

Biochemical investigations have shown:

(6) that differential gene activity in different tissues can be recognized by the differential synthesis of RNA molecules from different chromatin preparations

(7) that the specificity of masking of various regions of the DNA resides mainly in the acidic proteins of the chromosomes, and the restriction of transcription to specific regions of the DNA seems to be a consequence of interactions between both the histones and the acidic proteins.

(8) Histones are a very homogenous family of molecules, but since each may be reversibly phosphorylated and/or acetylated they possess sufficient versatility of structure to assist in the regulation of gene activity — and

(9) the effect of ecdysone on the puffing patterns of polytene chromosomes and of cyclic-AMP on histone phosphorylation, suggests ways in which the chromosome may respond to metabolic and environmental signals.

The chromosome is best regarded as an organelle whose function is the controlled and specific production of RNA molecules. It is thus the organelle most immediately concerned in the processes of cell differentiation and an understanding of its structure and mode of operation would enormously advance our understanding of cell differentiation as a whole.

4.2 RNA synthesis

Studies on the nature of the RNA molecules synthesized by bacterial polymerases using chromatin templates have been criticized on the grounds that it is not clear whether the RNA molecules so made, correspond to translatable sequences. Under the normal conditions of measuring transcription from chromatin preparations it is clear that only base sequences present in relatively high concentrations would be able to give rise to detectable amounts of RNA. The relationship between such reiterated sequences of DNA and a structural gene must be clarified before the true significance of much of the work reported in Section 4.1.4 can be determined.

When a pulse of a radioactive precursor of RNA is given to a eukaryote cell, it is rapidly incorporated into a heterogenous family of high molecular weight RNA molecules present in the nucleus (HnRNA). These molecules have a very short half life and little of the radioactivity that they acquire in a pulse-chase experiment is found in the cytoplasm until the HnRNA molecules have turned over several times. It is not clear what relationship these molecules have to mRNA, which must, in eukaryotes, be transported to the cytoplasm before being translated. They could, conceivably, have a control function [11a] and have nothing to do with mRNA as such, at all. Analysis of the cytoplasmic fate of isotope from RNA precursors in pulse-chase experiments has also shown that when it does appear in the cytoplasm the major part is in ribosomal RNA (rRNA) and not in mRNA. Thus several groups of workers have concentrated on the synthesis of specific RNA molecules, rather than RNA in general, in an attempt to determine which factors control differential RNA synthesis in differentiating cells.

The obvious specific RNA molecules to select for study initially are those found in ribosomes since these are generally reasonably stable and they are present in large amounts in most cells.

4.2.1 Ribosomal RNA synthesis

When cells are stained with reagents specific for RNA molecules a distinct entity — the nucleolus — in the nucleus stains very deeply. The nucleolus can often be seen in living cells using a phase contrast microscope and is probably present in most eukaryote cells. It is associated with a special portion of the chromatin which may penetrate into the substance of the nucleolus and which appears as a constriction (the nucleolus organiser) on a part of one or more chromosomes during division, when the nucleolus itself disappears. Nuclei have at least as many nucleoli as they have nucleolar organisers and some have many more. Many lines of evidence suggest that the nucleolar organiser is the part of the chromosome that carries the ribosomal genes and that the synthesis of ribosomes is associated with the nucleolus. As usual the most compelling evidence comes from the analysis of the appropriate mutants, in this case of *Xenopus laevis*.

A mutant strain of this organism was discovered in 1958 which had one nucleolus per cell instead of the normal two. Such organisms were designated 1-nu and are phenotypically normal, sexually competent adults. Embryos from the cross 1-nu X 1-nu consist of three types of individual: homozygous wild type (2-nu), heterozygous mutant (1-nu) and homozygous mutant (0-nu) in the ratio 1:2:1. The 0-nu mutants die at or soon after the early swimming larval stage. When the late gastrulae produced in the 1-nu X 1-nu cross were exposed to $^{14}CO_2$ for 20 h. and then transferred to normal medium containing $^{12}CO_2$ for a further 2 days (a pulse-chase experiment) and the nucleic acid content of each type of embryo analysed by sucrose density gradient centrifugation it was found that the 0-nu embryos had no radioactive rRNA as shown in Fig. 4.3. This experiment suggests that the genetic information needed for synthesising rRNA molecules is

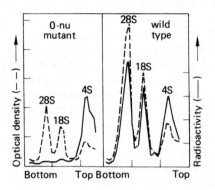

Fig. 4.3 RNA Synthesised in normal and mutant *Xenopus* embryos analysed by sucrose density centrifugation, (after Brown, 1966)

absent or dormant in the 0-nu embryos. Hybridisation of rRNA isolated from the wild type organisms with DNA isolated from 2-nu, 1-nu and 0-nu embryos showed that the genes for rRNA were indeed absent from 0-nu individuals and thus that the nucleolar organiser contains these genes (Fig. 4.4). Measurement of the amount of DNA in the form of a DNA-RNA hybrid at saturation (Fig. 4.4) with wild type DNA shows that some 0·07% of the normal diploid complement has a base composition complementary to that of rRNA. A diploid nucleus contains about 6 pg. (= 6×10^{-12} g.) of DNA which is equivalent to $3·6 \times 10^{12}$ daltons (one hydrogen atom weighs one dalton) and 0·07% of this is $2·5 \times 10^9$ daltons. The molecular weight of 28S rRNA is about $1·6 \times 10^6$ daltons and so a diploid nucleus of *Xenopus* contains approximately $2·5/1·6 \times 10^3$ or 1600 copies of the rRNA genes.

Essentially similar experiments to these with *Xenopus* have been done with the similar 'bobbed' mutants of *Drosophila* with essentially the same results.

In Fig. 4.3 it can be seen that although the

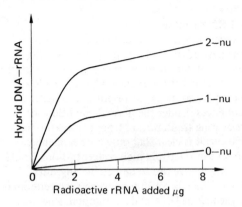

Fig. 4.4 Hybridisation of increasing amounts of *Xenopus* rRNA with a constant amount of DNA from the wild type and mutant embryos.

0-nu mutant embryos do not have any radioactive rRNA they do have rRNA. Thus although the cells of this mutant cannot make rRNA they contain ribosomes. The only source of these ribosomes is the egg, and analysis of *Xenopus* eggs shows that these have a very large number of ribosomes. This suggests that the oocyte would be the cell of choice for the study of rRNA synthesis and so it has proved.

rRNA synthesis is maximal in immature oocytes which are in the pachytene and diplotene stages of meiosis. During pachytene (which lasts for some weeks in oocytes) a 'nuclear cap' appears over the nucleus. Highly radioactive rRNA obtained from cultured *Xenopus* cells can be used as a cytological reagent to locate DNA sequences complementary to rRNA (see p. 20), and these techniques have shown the nuclear cap to contain numerous copies of such rDNA sequences [12]. The pachytene stage is followed by the diplotene stage (when the chromosomes adopt the lampbrush conformation), and at this time the nuclear cap disappears and about 1,000 nucleoli appear and cluster over the inner surface of the nuclear membrane. The oocyte stays in this arrested diplotene stage for months and it is at this stage that the cytoplasm enlarges and the bulk of the ribosomal content of the mature egg is synthesised.

A pachytene nucleus contains about 12 pg. of chromosomal DNA (4 X the haploid content, Table 2 p. 19) but the nuclear cap it produces contains about 30 pg. of rDNA. This represents an extraordinarily large degree of specific gene amplification, and hybridisation studies with rRNA and oocyte DNA have suggested that at least 10^6 copies of the rRNA genes are present in such oocytes. This means that oocyte DNA should be enriched for rDNA and density gradient analysis of DNA preparations from oocytes shows that they do, in fact, have a nuclear satellite of higher G + C content than the main band DNA (Fig. 4.5) which contains sequences complementary to those of rRNA [13]. However

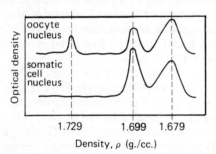

Fig. 4.5 Density gradient analysis of DNA from nuclei of somatic and oocyte cells of *Xenopus laevis* showing rDNA ($\rho = 1\cdot729$) main band DNA ($\rho = 1\cdot699$) and marker DNA ($\rho = 1\cdot679$). Redrawn from [13].

the G + C content of this satellite differs from that of rRNA so there must be some other DNA besides that complementary to rRNA. This DNA is called 'spacer' DNA and separates one tandem pair of genes for the 18S and 28S RNA molecules, from other such tandem pairs. Miller and Beatty [14] have spread nucleoli carefully

on an electron microscope grid and visualized the process of transciption (Fig. 4.6). The 'spacer' DNA can be clearly seen as the untranscribed region between two arrow-head structures each of which represents about 100 polymerase molecules attached to the DNA and actively engaged in synthesising RNA. The exact function of the spacer DNA is unknown but two closely related and interbreeding species of *Xenopus, X. mulleri* and *X. laevis* which have rRNA molecules of identical sequence, have spacer DNA regions with very different base composition.

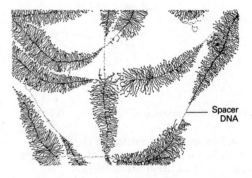

Spacer
DNA

Fig. 4.6 Drawing of electron microscope visualization of ribosomal genes of the newt, being transcribed; about X 20,000. Redrawn from [14].

In Fig. 4.6 it can be seen that all the transcribed genes appear to be the same length, although the ribosomes of *Xenopus* contain three species of RNA (5S, 18S and 28S). The 5S genes are not coded for by genes in the nucleolar organiser region of the DNA, and so the absence of a short arrow head formation is not too surprising, and the absence of two sizes of large arrow head is due to the fact that the 18S and 28S RNA molecules are the end products of a complex of post-transcriptional modification reactions of a 35S molecule whose synthesis is in fact visualised in Fig. 4.6.

Careful analysis of the path taken by isotopes

45

in pulse-chase experiments using tissue culture cells first suggested that rRNA molecules were synthesised by paths which were complex and species specific. RNA molecules differ in base sequence, secondary structure and size and the last two properties have been exploited in developing electrophoretic techniques of high resolving power. Using these techniques if has been shown that in *Xenopus* the pathway of rRNA synthesis is probably as shown in Fig. 4.7 [15]. The pathway followed in other species seems to differ in detail although the ultimate size of the rRNA molecules is similar in all eukaryotes.

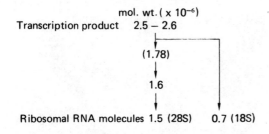

Transcription product

Fig. 4.7 Pathway of synthesis of rRNA molecules in *Xenopus*. The mol. wt. of molecules is given in millions. Redrawn from [15].

The reason for these post-transcriptional modifications is unknown but they are obviously of great significance since in *Xenopus* about 15% of the initial transcription product is degraded (in mammals it appears to be as high as 50%) and this must represent a considerable 'waste' of metabolic energy.

It is difficult to account for the selective amplification of the rDNA in oocytes. Two possible explanations have been suggested. The first is that this reflects the fact that RNA polymerase molecules can only synthesise RNA at a finite rate and if there were only four times the haploid number of copies of the ribosomal genes in the diplotene nuclei then it would be impossible to make sufficient ribosomes to allow the oocyte to complete its maturation in

the time available. This may be so (the detailed calculations are quite convincing) but it does not explain why there is no specific amplification of the genes for the 5S RNA molecule of the ribosomal proteins. If these are present in a suitably amplified state in the oocyte then, on this argument, they must be grossly over-represented in somatic cells. The other explanation is that the nucleolar DNA is free of various restricting controls that prevents it being sufficiently active when integrated in the chromosome. The specific amplification of this DNA in oocytes is thus not only to increase the number of templates, but also to alter the control mechanisms. The rate of production of the 18S and 28S RNA molecules seems to control the rate of production of the 5S RNA molecule (itself the product of the post-transcriptional modification of a larger precursor) since the 0-nu embryos of *Xenopus* do not synthesize any 5S molecules although they have the required gene. If the synthesis of ribosomal proteins is controlled in similar fashion, then absence of specific amplification of these genes in oocytes might be accounted for.

Little is known of how the extent of the amplification of rDNA is controlled during oogenesis. Surveys of different amphibia have shown that although different species have widely different contents of DNA (Table 2, p. 19) their oocytes have approximately the same amount of extra rDNA and thus similar numbers of nucleoli. This suggests that there is a feedback type of control of the amplification process and in agreement with this is the observation that oocytes of 2-nu and 1-nu individuals of *Xenopus* have identical amounts of rDNA, although 1-nu cells have lost half their nucleolar organisers.

Amphibian eggs can be regarded as cells specialised for the storage of (amongst other things) ribosomes, and the specific amplification of their ribosomal genes can be viewed as an expression of this differentiated function. It is interesting now to ask if this is a general response of cells during their differentiation; do, for example, erythrocytes whose differentiated function is to make and store the protein haemoglobin make numerous copies of the genes for the haemoglobin polypeptides during erythropoeisis?

4.2.2 Messenger RNA synthesis

mRNA was first characterized in prokaryotes as a labile high molecular weight RNA fraction and much of the initial work exploited pulse-chase experiments to follow mRNA synthesis and behaviour. Similar experiments with eukaryotes led to the characterisation of HnRNA (p. 42) which was often assumed to be mRNA. However, since little of the HnRNA ever appears in the cytoplasm (where mRNA has to be translated) this identification cannot be correct and has led to great confusion.

mRNA, by definition, is an RNA molecule which carries the transcribed code for the primary structure of a protein to the cytoplasm. Such molecules must therefore be found in the cytoplasm as component parts of the polysomes — they must indeed be the molecule which holds the individual ribosomes of the polysomes together. When it became apparent that attempts to characterise the mRNA molecules at the time of their synthesis in the nucleus using pulses of radioactive precursors, were giving confusing results, attempts were made to characterise mRNA at its site of translation — the polysome. Most cells make numerous proteins and therefore have a wide variety of polysomes in their cytoplasms. In order to obtain a reasonably homogenous polysome preparation from which it would be reasonable to attempt to isolate mRNA, it is necessary to have a population of cells making predominantly one kind of protein. Three kinds of such cells have been studied intensively so far: the immature erythrocyte (reticulocyte) of rabbits or birds, which makes predominantly haemoglobin [16];

the embryonic muscle cells of chick which make tropomyosin, myosin and actin [17]; and the early cleavage stages of the sea urchin which make histones [18]. In all these cases essentially similar experiments have been (or are being) done.

The cells are lysed under conditions which preserve the rather fragile polysome structures, and the lysates are centrifuged through a sucrose gradient and the polysomes collected and concentrated. In the case of reticulocytes where haemoglobin is the predominant protein, there is only one polysome peak, in the case of embryonic muscle the proteins are of such different sizes that three discrete polysome peaks are obtained, each enriched for the appropriate mRNA (Fig. 4.8) and in the case of the sea urchin the

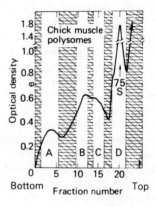

Fig. 4.8 Sucrose gradient analysis of polysomes from 14-day embryonic chick limb buds. Redrawn from [17].

small size of the histones (and hence their mRNA's) means that the histone mRNA is found in the small polysome region of the gradient, separated from most other polysomes. At best some 0·5% of these polysome preparations will be mRNA, the rest being rRNA and various proteins and peptides. The problem is thus to separate the nucleic acids from the proteins and

47

then to separate the mRNA from rRNA. In principle since the haemoglobin and histone mRNA's should be about 10S this should be relatively straight forward, but in practice it is difficult to avoid degradation of the mRNA by nucleases and thus families of molecules are obtained. The best preparations of haemoglobin mRNA contain two molecular species (as would be expected since haemoglobin has two different polypeptide chains α and β) which are both about 10S and contain about 100 nucleotides in excess of the number required to code for the primary sequence of the α or β chains. These mRNA preparations will support the synthesis of globin even in heterologous systems using ribosomes and enzymes from a source different from the source of mRNA. It seems clear, therefore, that they are in fact mRNA molecules. Similarly the mRNA's obtained from embryonic muscle and the cleavage stages of sea urchins will support the *in vitro* synthesis of the muscle proteins and histones respectively. Hybridisation experiments carried out with the histone mRNA [19], and the haemoglobin mRNA [20] have given different extents of gene reiteration. DNA-RNA hybridisation experiments have been carried out in conditions of DNA excess and have suggested that each sea urchin cell has about 400 copies of the histone genes whereas the reticulocyte cannot have more than 10, probably has less than 5, and most probably has only two copies of the haemoglobin genes. These results suggest that gene amplification of the type seen in oocytes for rDNA does not occur generally.

The ribosomal genes of oocytes are probably amplified several thousand fold because of the necessity of making a lot of rRNA in a relatively short time (p. 45) but this argument cannot be used with the same force in the case of proteins since the synthesis of more than one mRNA molecule from the appropriate structural gene is equivalent to amplifying it (Fig. 4.9). This does not mean, of course, that gene amplification of protein structural genes does not occur, it clearly does in the case of the histone genes of sea urchins, but it does suggest that the controls over the synthesis of rRNA might be different from those over the synthesis of mRNA.

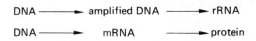

Fig. 4.9 Transcription of genes coding for proteins is equivalent to amplification of ribosomal genes.

Attempts to purify the DNA primed RNA polymerase enzyme of eukaryotes has shown that several protein species have this activity. They may be distinguished on the basis of their co-factor requirements and sensitivity to various inhibitors and the relative amounts of each species changes during the early stages of embryogenesis in the sea urchin, as the pattern of RNA synthesis changes from being predominantly a synthesis of mRNA at the cleavage stages, to being both mRNA and rRNA at the late gastrula stages. Thus different enzymes may also be involved in the synthesis of these two different classes of RNA.

The initial transcription product of the rDNA is considerably larger than the finally fully processed rRNA molecules. The haemoglobin mRNA molecules contain regions which are not translated and so the initial transcription products of the structural genes of proteins may also be larger than needed solely to code for the primary structure of the protein. There is some evidence that part of the base sequence of some of the HnRNA molecules is identical with the base sequence of some mRNA moleucles and so it seems likely that mRNA molecules are the end products of a post-transcriptional processing mechanism, which results in only a fraction of the initial transcription product reaching the cytoplasm. Nothing is known of this process but if it exists it clearly provides another point at which control mechanisms of great significance for cell differentiation might occur. There is some evidence that in the cellular slime mould RNA molecules made in the presence of inhibitors of protein synthesis are unstable, suggesting that proteins are involved in the modification processes, and cell fusion experiments between cells such as the erythrocyte and HeLa tissue culture cells, have implicated the nucleolus in mRNA transport as well as rRNA synthesis [21]. This is not unreasonable since what is needed in the cytoplasm is polysomes rather than mRNA as such and so it is logical for ribosome synthesis and transport to the cytoplasm to be linked to mRNA synthesis and transport. Finally, there is direct evidence that in at least the cleavage stage of embryos of sea urchins and some fish, mRNA and protein are combined in a specific association to form 20-65S particles called 'informosomes'. These particles appear in the cytoplasm where they are converted into polysomes by a process which might be long delayed and is obviously subject to some unknown control mechanisms. Eggs seem to contain a large store of informosomes and inactive polysomes which become activated by a proteolytic attack following fertilization [22]. It is likely that the whole sequence of steps resulting in the modification of the initial transcription product, its incorporation into a particle for transport to the cytoplasm and its final appearance in a polysome will shortly be understood now that purified mRNA's are becoming available. At the moment there are tantalizing hints that initiation complexes between mRNA and ribosomal sub-units analogous to those of prokaryotes can be formed [23], and that runs of adenine residues seem to characterize mRNA [24], but the significance and generality of these findings remain to be established.

4.3 Protein synthesis
Proteins synthesized during cell differentiation are either enzymes needed in increased amounts or, more rarely, not needed previously, or they are structural proteins needed for the construction of novel cytological structures and for export to other cells. Our knowledge of the way in which these two classes of proteins are synthesized is both incomplete and biased in favour of the 'structural' or non-enzymic class.

Protein secreting cells are characterized by an elaborate system of rough endoplasmic reticulum. The polysomes (whose presence gives the 'roughness' to the endoplasmic reticulum) are attached to the membrane surface by their large 60S subunits. As the protein is made it is secreted into the lumen of the reticulum. There is evidence that the membrane contains an enzyme which catalyzes the formation or reformation of disulphide.bridges and the final conformation of the molecule is probably not achieved until it is in the lumen. The rough endoplasmic reticulum is part of the same system of tubules and sheets as is the smooth endoplasmic reticulum and the Golgi apparatus. The Golgi apparatus is concerned with 'packaging' material to be excreted into vesicles so that they may be transported to the cell membrane and thus to the exterior. Little is known of the nature of this packaging process but since many secreted proteins are glycoproteins it seems that part of the function of the Golgi body is the addition and/or modification of the carbohydrate moieties of glycoproteins. A number of proteins, such as insulin, are made in the form of one polypeptide chain which is then specifically cleaved to give rise to the physiologically active, two chain, molecule. This post-translational modification of proteins is analogous to the post-transcriptional modification of RNA molecules and, if it occurs, seems to take place in or near the Golgi body. Finally, once the proteins are packaged into vesicles they move to the cell membrane where they fuse with the membrane and thus release their contents to the exterior. In some tissues there is only one direction in which this secretion can occur and it seems that in these cases the vesicles are guided by a system of microfilaments or microtubules so that they deposit their contents in the correct place. Thus in these cells protein synthesis must be coupled with the synthesis of, or development of, endoplasmic reticulum, Golgi apparatus and a system of microfilaments and microtubules. At the biochemical level there seems to be a coupling of protein synthesis and phospholipid synthesis in metamorphosing tadpoles but attempts to study the nature and implication of this coupling are only just beginning.

Not all cells differentiate into protein secreting cells but even those that do not, often make proteins which have to be incorporated into specific structures before they can be physiologically active. Thus in the liver of the metamorphosing tadpole, a new class of mitochondria appear that contain some of the urea cycle enzymes needed by the frog. These new mitochondria first appear localized at the perinuclear region of the cell where there is also an extensive proliferation of the endoplasmic reticulum. How these enzymes get from the reticulum to the mitochondria remains unknown, however.

The reticulocyte is the classic case of a cell which makes a protein, haemoglobin, which is neither secreted nor part of another structure but just exists in the cytoplasm. The polysomes that synthesise haemoglobin appear free in the reticulocyte cytoplasm and do not appear to be associated with any membrane system. Thus there is no necessary connection between polysome function and adsorption to a membrane surface and this, of course, makes it more likely that controls exist during differentiation which determine whether, or how, polysomes interact with membranes. Haemoglobin itself is a complex protein consisting of two different types of polypeptide chain, the complete molecule consisting of four polypeptides, four haem groups and four iron atoms. The assembly of

such a molecule implies a variety of controls over polysome function and that such things do exist is shown by the fact that genetically controlled defects in the assembly process of several proteins have been reported [2]. The uptake and metabolism of iron is closely controlled by a number of hormones and the synthesis of haem seems to be controlled by feedback inhibition by haemin (haem + iron) of the first unique enzyme in porphyrin biosynthesis (δ-amino laevulinate synthetase). Haemin, in turn, stimulates globin synthesis by promoting the initiation of translation of the mRNA's for both the α and β polypeptides and completed α chains appear to interact with the β chains whilst the latter are still polysome bound. This interaction seems to have some regulatory significance since α chains not so bound, appear to be rapidly degraded. These $\alpha\beta$ sub-units combine with haemin as they are released from the polysome and by sequential addition of $\alpha\beta$ sub-units and haem groups, a haemoglobin molecule is formed [25]. Thus the synthesis of haemoglobin involves controls at a number of different levels, but the way in which these interact in time (to allow for the switch in synthesis from foetal to adult forms) and in space (to ensure that only the appropriate cells make haemoglobin), is unknown.

In many cases there is an alteration in level of an enzyme during cell differentiation rather than the *de novo* synthesis of a protein not previously made as in the case of haemoglobin. Little is known of the way in which such subtle changes occur but it seems that they are often achieved, not only by alterations in the rate at which enzymes are synthesized, but by alterations in the rates at which they are degraded.

4.4 Protein degradation
Studies with model systems have suggested that the loss of an enzyme is as significant an event as is the acquisition of an enzyme during cell differentiation. However, despite the evident

50

importance of selective loss of proteins, little is known of the biochemical mechanisms whereby this selective loss is achieved. Surprisingly, most of what is known about selective protein degradation has come, not from model systems where it might be imagined that this process would be peculiarily susceptible to analysis, but from studies on the induction of enzymes in the mammalian liver. The liver is peculiarily exposed to environmental changes since it receives its blood supply direct from the portal vein which drains the intestine. Thus the liver operates in an environment which constantly changes in chemical composition as food is digested and absorbed. The liver is also responsible for maintaining the concentration of many metabolites in the blood supply to other tissues and it is thus also sensitive to a variety of hormonal stimuli. It has been found that levels of many liver enzymes are extremely sensitive to changes in dietary regime, hormonal balance in the blood stream, and metabolite levels in the portal vein. However, enzyme induction differs in one important and fundamental respect from similar inductions in populations of bacterial cells, namely that when the inducer is removed from an exponentially growing population of bacteria, the enzyme induced prior to removal of inducer is stable in the absence of inducer, whereas the converse is true of the liver (Fig. 4.10). This is not altogether surprising since the bacterial cell is rapidly dividing and can 'dilute out' the induced enzyme, whereas the liver cell has a life span of 160-400 days and so cannot rapidly dilute out an induced enzyme. It is interesting that when bacteria cease to grow (and so can no longer dilute out materials) protein turnover is initiated and induced enzymes are now degraded.

The decrease of enzyme activity seen in Fig. 4.9, might be due to the conversion of the enzyme to an inactive form or due to the actual degradation of the enzyme molecule to amino acids. Cases of enzyme activation/inactivation

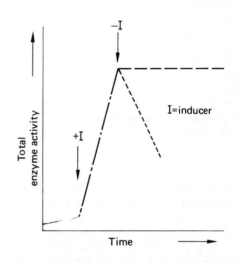

Fig. 4.10 Diagrammatic time course of enzyme induction in bacterial cells (− − −) and mammalian liver (· · ·) showing different stabilities of induced enzymes.

under the influence of 'inducers/repressors' are known and will be discussed in Section 4.6, but addition of radioactive amino acids to an animal's diet followed by the return of that animal to a nonradioactive diet and analysis of the rate of loss of radioactivity from the various components of the liver, has shown that there is also a marked heterogeneity in the turnover of the cellular constituents and thus actual degradation of the enzyme molecule can occur. In Table 4 it can be seen that the half-lives of various enzymes and organelles vary considerably and are in some cases much less than the generation time of the cells. It is clear that the turnover is an intracellular process and is not due to the turnover of the cells as a whole. The range of half-lives further suggests that this process is specific and highly regulated. Thus an inducer might cause an apparent change in the specific activity of a liver enzyme, not only by increasing the rate of

51

Table 4. Turnover rates of components of rat liver cells (from 26).

cell fraction or enzyme	$t_{1/2}$ (days)
whole homogenate	3·3
nucleus	5·1
mitochondria	6·8
lyosomes	7·1
supernatant	5·1
plasma membrane	1·8
glutamate/alanine transaminase	2-3
tyrosine transaminase	0·1
catalase	1·4
arginase	4·5

its synthesis but also by altering the rate of its degradation. A particularily clear-cut case of different inducers acting in these two different ways is the induction of tryptophan pyrollase (or oxygenase) studied by Schimke and his colleagues whose work, and the whole topic of control of enzyme levels in mammalian tissues, is reviewed in [26].

The specific activity of tryptophan pyrollase in the livers of adrenalectomized rats can be increased both by the injection of tryptophan and hydrocortisone (Fig. 4.11) and, since these two inducers act synergistically, it seems probable that they act by different mechanisms. The tryptophan pyrollase molecules synthesized by either inducer, were shown to be immunologically identical, and the increases in specific activity were similarly shown to be due to alterations in the amount of immunologically active protein synthesized. Measurement of ^{14}C-leucine incorporation rates into both the soluble protein fraction of the cell and specifically the tryptophan pyrrolase molecule showed that whereas tryptophan injection has no effect on the rate of synthesis of the enzyme, hydro-cortisone injection increases the rate of synthesis of this enzyme specifically. This suggests that tryptophan must affect the rate of degradation of tryptophan pyrollase and direct tests of this hypothesis have shown it to be correct (Fig.

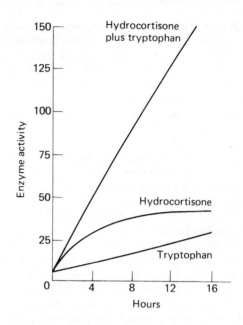

Fig. 4.11 Induction of tryptophan pyrollase by tryptophan and hydrocortisone in adrenalectomized rats. Redrawn from [26].

4.12). Thus of the two inducers of this enzyme one acts by increasing the rate of synthesis (hydrocortisone) and the other acts by decreasing the rate of degradation (tryptophan). Virtually nothing is known of the molecular details of this degradation process except that it is highly specific. The extraordinary specificity of the degradation process is illustrated by analysis of the levels of catalase in the liver and kidney of a number of in-bred mouse strains. In the 1920's a mutation occurred in a colony of mice at the Rockefeller Institute, New York. The descendants of this mutant comprise the C57 and C58 strains of mice which have only half the normal specific activity of catalase in their kidneys and liver. The subsequent history of these mice is well reviewed in [2] and is a fascinating example of the often inconsequential

52

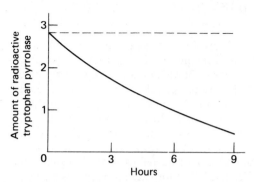

Fig. 4.12 Effect of tryptophan on the stability of tryptophan pyrollase *in vivo*. Rats containing radioactive enzyme were injected at t = 0 with saline (—) or tryptophan (– – –). Redrawn from [26].

path of scientific research. In the 1940's the C57 strain of mice gave rise to another strain which had regained the normal liver catalase activity but had still only half the normal catalese activity in the kidney. Studies of the genetics of these two mutations and biochemical studies of the purified catalases of the two strains and their rates of synthesis and degradation have shown that at least two genes are involved in determining the catalase activity of any tissue. One is the Cs gene which is the structural gene for the catalase protein, and it was a mutation in this gene which gave rise to the C57 and C58 strains. This mutation was such as to alter the catalytic activity of the molecule to 1/2 the normal — hence the change in specific activity. The second gene Ce controls the rate of degradation of the catalase protein in the liver (but not the kidney). A mutation in this gene gave rise to the second set of mutants whose normal catalase level in the liver is due, not to a restoration of the catalytic efficiency of the catalase protein, but to a halving in the rate of degradation of the catalase in the liver and thus a doubling in the number of catalase molecules

present. The implications of this work are that the degradation system is specific for one protein (catalase) and is also tissue-specific in its expression. All the proteins in the liver turnover, and if each had a specific protein which controlled the rate of its degradation there would be the logically ridiculous situation in which a protein would be required to degrade a protein to degrade a protein. . . . ad inf. Schemes can be devised whereby the Ce gene controls some lysosomal recognition site which would be responsible for absorbing a number of proteins with binding constants which varied according to their individual structures (which would mean that the tertiary structure of a protein determined its half life), but in the absence of any information such speculations are perhaps not very profitable. Tissue specific factors have also been implicated in the control of the rate of degradation of lactate dehydrogenase so the problem is a general one.

The tissue-specific control of the degradation of a protein is an extreme example of the modification of an enzymic activity to fit it for a new cellular environment. There are other, less drastic, tissue specific modification mechanisms known, and it is to these that we must now turn.

4.5 Protein modification
When enzymes are purified from cells it is not uncommon to find that several distinct and separable protein species have the same catalytic activity. Such molecules are called isoenzymes or isozymes, and at least 100 enzymic activities are known to exist in multiple molecular forms. Isoenzymes can arise as a result of many different mechanisms which involve either enzyme catalysed modifications of some sort, or they represent time or tissue-dependent changes in the protein synthetic pattern.

Haemoglobin is not strictly an enzyme but it represents a clear example of the time-dependent change in isoenzyme pattern. At least four structural genes are known to code for the

53

synthesis of haemoglobin polypeptides, α, β, γ, δ. These genes function at different stages in the development of the organism and their relative activity determines the relative abundance of different haemoglobin molecules. In foetal mammals haemoglobin has the composition $\alpha_2\gamma_2$ but at about the time of birth the composition changes to $\alpha_2\beta_2$ with a few percent of the total being $\alpha_2\delta_2$..The altered pattern of gene activity is itself genetically controlled and can be altered by mutation. In the disease thalassemia there is an inability to initiate the production of β chains and consequently no $\alpha_2\beta_2$ moleucles are produced. Instead the individuals survive by continuing to produce $\alpha_2\gamma_2$ molecules and by overproducing $\alpha_2\delta_2$ molecules. Such individuals suffer from anaemia since their blood has a reduced capacity to carry oxygen due to the fact that the $\alpha_2\gamma_2$ molecules are not so well adapted to the air-breathing, adult stage of life as is the $\alpha_2\beta_2$ molecule. Conversely the $\alpha_2\gamma_2$ molecule is better adapted to the demands of foetal oxygen carriage from the maternal to foetal blood systems than is the $\alpha_2\beta_2$ molecules. The amino acid sequences of the β and γ polypeptides are similar (they have almost certainly arisen by gene duplication followed by divergent evolution) and thus the existence of 'isoenzymes' of haemoglobin represents a sophisticated and elegant solution to the changing physiological requirements of the developing organism.

In the case of lactate dehydrogenase (LDH) there is not only a time-dependent change in the isoenzyme pattern, but also a tissue dependent change. Like haemoglobin, LDH is a tetramer containing two different types of polypeptides but, unlike haemoglobin, the two polypeptides (called A and B chains) can combine together in any proportions to produce the enzymatically active tetramer. Thus there exist five possible types of LDH with polypeptide compositions:

$$\text{LDH-1} = B_4, \text{LDH-2} = A_1B_3, \text{LDH-3} = A_2B_2$$
$$\text{LDH-4} = A_3B_1 \text{ and LDH-5} = A_4.$$

and if these molecules have the same thermodynamic stability (as they appear to) then the proportions in which the various isoenzymes of LDH occur in a cell should represent the relative proportions of A and B chains present at the time of assembly. LDH isoenzymes can be separated on starch gels by electrophoresis and the position of each enzymatically active molecule is readily detected using a cytological stain (Fig. 4.13). The formazan produced is highly

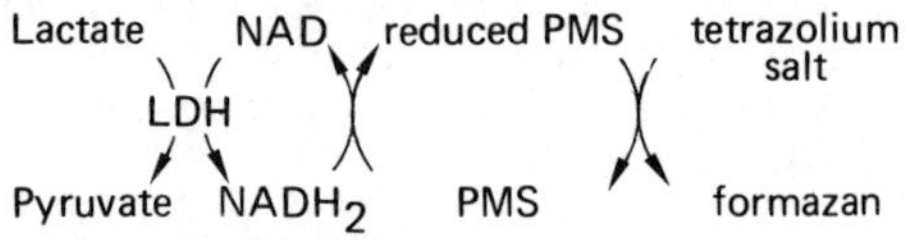

overall reaction:

Lactate + tetrazolium salt = pyruvate + formazan.

Fig. 4.13 Cytological stain for LDH activity. PMS = phenazine methyl sulphate, an artificial electron carrier.

coloured and insoluble and the sensitivity and convenience of this procedure has meant that numerous tissue extracts can be quickly and reliably assayed for their content of LDH enzymes (Fig. 4.14). The size of the stained portion of the gel is proportional to the concentration of each isoenzyme, and it can be seen that the distribution is very different in different tissues. If the LDH-1 and LDH-5 isoenzymes are isolated from such gels, mixed in the ratio of 1:1 and then disocciated by freezing in buffer and allowed to reassociate by gentle thawing, a mixture of all 5 isoenzymes is found in the ratio of 1:4:6:4:1, as would be expected for the random combination of A and B chains present in equal proportions. When the relative abundancies of different isoenzymes in different tissues are determined accurately, it is usually found that the proportions are indeed binomials

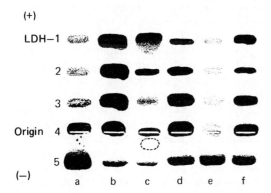

Fig. 4.14 Distribution of LDH isoenzymes in a number of tissues of the rat. (a) skeletal muscle, (b) heart muscle, (c) testis, (d) tongue, (e) lung, (f) brain. Redrawn from [27].

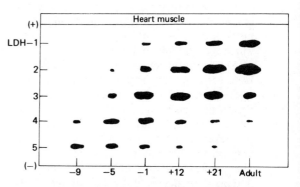

Fig. 4.15 Changes in the LDH isoenzyme pattern in the heart tissues of the developing mouse. At the extreme left is the pattern from an embryo 9 days before birth, at the extreme right the adult pattern. Birth occurs at O. Redrawn from [27].

but skewed from the 1:4:6:4:1 ratio, suggesting that random combination of A and B chains is occurring but that the A and B chains are not present in equal amounts. From patterns such as that of Fig. 4.14 the relative activities of the genes coding for the A and B chains can therefor be deduced.

Studies of the isoenzyme patterns of the same tissue at different times in development, have also shown that there are time and tissue-dependent changes in the isoenzyme pattern (Fig. 4.15) so the distributions seen in the adult are but the last stages in a sequence of characteristic changes which occur during cell differentiation. The reproducibility of these changes suggests that each of the different isoenzymes plays its own particular role not only in the adult cells, but also in each of the various stages

during the development of the final cell type. In post-pubertal testis tissue an additional isoenzyme is found in most vertebrate species (Fig. 4.14, c in the ringed position). The appearance of this enzyme is associated with the production of spermatocytes and it seems to play a specific role in spermatogenesis since eggs and early cleavage stages have only LDH-1. This extra isoenzyme LDH_x appears to have a third type of polypeptide chain and its synthesis shows the clear connection between change in isoenzyme pattern and change in cell function.

The change in the haemoglobin content of organisms as they develop can be accounted for in terms of the changing physiological environment and the fact that different haemoglobins differ in the nature of their oxygen binding reactions. In the same way it is reasonable to explain the changes in isoenzyme pattern seen

55

during cell differentiation as reflecting different cellular environments and/or different metabolic requirements during the differentiation process. Kinetic experiments have shown that LDH-1 and LDH-5 differ markedly in the extent to which they react with analogues of NAD, in their K_m's for various substrates and the variations of these with pH and in the extent to which they are inhibited by pyruvate.

At a pyruvate concentration of $0\cdot01\ M$ LDH-1 is about 80% inhibited whereas LDH-5 still retains 100% of its activity. A physiological significance has been claimed for this observation since it is known that skeletal muscle pyruvate concentrations can vary widely, whereas heart muscle pyruvate concentrations are much more constant – and LDH-1 is the predominant isoenzyme of heart tissue and LDH-5 of skeletal muscle (Fig. 4.14, a and b). However, although very attractive, this theory has been criticised on the grounds that this difference in sensitivity to pyruvate inhibition is only seen when very dilute enzyme solutions are studied (about $10^{-8}M$). When enzyme concentrations are used which are more nearly those found in cells (about $10^{-5}M$), then this difference in pyruvate inhibition is not observed [28]. The finding that kinetic constants are not in fact constant but are dependent on the enzyme concentration, undermines much of the physiological significance and usefulness of enzyme kinetic studies. These are usually carried out at low enzyme concentrations ($10^{-7}-10^{-9}M$) and high substrate concentrations ($10^{-3}-10^{-1}M$), whereas it is becoming clear that intracellular conditions are such that enzyme concentrations and substrate and effector concentrations are comparable (about $10^{-5}M$) for major metabolic pathways, [29]. It will be interesting to see whether the major reinvestigation of the kinetic properties of enzymes which ought thus to be undertaken, will lead to any significant rethinking of accepted biochemical theories – if the LDH situation is typical it clearly might.

The A and B polypeptides of LDH have, as far as is known, no intrinsic enzyme activity. However other cases are known in which two proteins interact, so altering their enzyme properties, but where at least one of the interacting proteins is enzymically active in its own right. Perhaps the best understood case of this type is the enzyme lactose synthetase [30]. Lactose synthetase is found in the lactating mammary gland of mammals where it catalyses the reaction: UDP-galactose + glucose = lactose + UDP. It consists of two subunits (called, inevitably, the A and B subunits). The A subunit is itself an enzyme and it is present in all endoplasmic reticulum membranes where it catalyses the synthesis of substituted lactosamine units which are themselves part of the structure of many glycoproteins. It can be assayed *in vitro* by the reaction: UDP-galactose + N-acetylglucosamine = UDP + N-acetyllactosamine. The B subunit is also known to exist independently in milk where it is known as α-lactalbumin, the major component of whey. The α-lactalbumin or B subunit has no known intrinsic activity but it inhibits the N-acetyllactosamine activity of the A protein and activates its lactose synthetase activity. The mammary glands are derived, in the anatomical and evolutionary sense, from the sebaceous glands of the skin and thus their cells would be expected to have an extensive membrane system suitable for secretory purposes. During the latter stages of pregnancy there is an extensive proliferation of this membrane system and with this there is an extensive synthesis of the A protein which is needed for the synthesis of the glycoproteins of the membranes. This process is controlled by the interaction of the hormones insulin, hydrocortisone and prolactin and can be mimicked *in vitro* in tissue culture. At birth the progesterone level in the mother's blood stream declines and this coincides with a massive synthesis of the B subunit (α-lactalbumin). This protein is secreted after synthesis into the lumen of the endoplasmic reticulum and is thence transported to the Golgi body where it is packaged into vesicles whose walls contain the A protein. Lactose synthesis can now ensue and the final fluid excreted by the cell contains both lactose and α-lactalbumin. The whole system represents an extraordinarily sophisticated example of the way in which protein-protein interactions can modify enzyme activity and ensure the balanced synthesis of lactose and α-lactalbumin for milk production. It also represents a system in which hormones play key roles in the control of membrane proliferation, protein synthesis and control of carbohydrate metabolism. Perhaps most intriguing of all, however, has been the discovery that the amino acid sequence of α-lactalbumin is virtually identical to that of lysozyme, an enzyme present in tears which degrades the murein component of bacterial cell walls. Model building studies have suggested that the tertiary structure of α-lactalbumin and lysozyme are extremely similar and it seems clear that these two proteins must be derived from a common ancestral polypeptide. This finding may be rationalized, of course, since lysozyme is also the product of a modified sebaceous gland and its substrate has chemical affinities to lactose and so on; but no biochemist would have been so bold as to have predicted this similarity in structure before its discovery — which suggests that surprises await both those interested in cell differentiation and those interested in evolution as more protein structures are elucidated in the future.

Isoenzymes can also be formed by the modification of intact proteins. The addition of carbohydrate residues to proteins in the Golgi body has been mentioned before (p. 49), and whole families of glycoproteins can be produced by the modification of the carbohydrate moiety by glycosidase or other enzyme activities. Similarly, changes in the redox state of a protein, as in the case of malate dehydrogenase, and deamidation of glutamine and asparagine residues, as in the case of the proteins of the lens of the eye, can give rise to multiple forms of biologically active proteins.

In some cases, of course, isoenzymes have nothing in common and differ in amino acid composition and sequence. There are also an increasing number of cases in which there are reversible enzyme-catalysed phosphorylations, adenylations, acetylations and other similar alterations in the covalent structure of enzymes. These changes often cause consequent changes in the polymeric state of the enzyme but since they are usually readily reversible and are of considerable significance in altering the metabolic behaviour of the enzyme, they are best considered in the context of the control of metabolism rather than the control of protein structure.

4.6 Metabolism and macromolecular synthesis. The synthesis of a novel cellular component during differentiation is rarely an end in itself, but rather the means chosen to alter the metabolism of the cell so that its function may be changed appropriately. Of course, there are cases, such as the synthesis of haemoglobin and the muscle proteins, where the synthesis of a protein is largely an end in itself but usually there appears to be some connection between the altered metabolism of the cell and the differential gene activity that we have been discussing in this chapter. Thus in the case of the glycolytic enzymes (Fig. 4.16) there is a relationship between the amount of an enzyme present in a tissue and the maximal rate of glycolysis observed. However, the remarkable thing about Fig. 4.16 is that most of the enzymes are present in amounts 10-100 times the maximal rates of glycolysis. Of course, there can only be one rate-limiting step in a metabolic sequence at any one time but even the enzyme catalysing that is usually present in an apparently generous excess (phosphofructokinase is usually the rate limiting step in glycolysis). It is thus difficult to

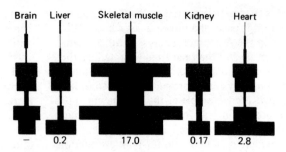

Hexokinase
Phosphofructokinase
Aldolase
Glyceraldehyde phosphate dehydrogenase
Phosphoglycerate kinase
Enolase
Pyruvate kinase
Lactate dehydrogenase
Maximal rate of glycolysis

	Brain	Liver	Skeletal muscle	Kidney	Heart
Maximal rate of glycolysis	−	0.2	17.0	0.17	2.8

Fig. 4.16 Activities of glycolytic enzymes in rat tissues. Enzyme activity is proportional to the width of the bar, the phosphofructokinase activity of heart muscle is 20 μmoles/min/g wet weight of tissue. Values for the maximal rates of glycolysis are also expressed in these units. Redrawn from [31].

rationalize the differential synthesis of the enzymes of Fig. 4.16 during the differentiation which led to the formation of the various tissues. The possibility that the presentation of the enzyme content of a cell in terms of its activity is misleading, is also suggested by the finding that the concentration of glycolytic intermediates during glycolysis oscillate in a stable fashion and an excess of some of the glycolytic enzymes appears to be essential for these oscillatory changes in concentration [32]. Thus what is important is not so much whether glycolysis occurs at a given rate or whether the glycolytic enzymes are efficiently utilized but rather that the glycolytic activity of the cell can be appropiately controlled and integrated into the overall metabolism of the cell. Interestingly, although there is no obvious relationship between the specific activity of the enzymes of glycolysis (Fig. 4.16), there does appear to be a relationship between the *amount* of each protein species synthesised. In fact, in yeast, the normalities of the glycolytic enzymes (the normality = molar concentration of enzyme/ number of substrate binding sites) appear to be ordered in simple numerical proportions $(1:2:4:8)$ over the range $2 \cdot 5 - 20 \times 10^{-5} N$ [32]. Thus what may be controlled and important is the amount of protein made , and its

catalytic activity then becomes of secondary importance provided, of course, a certain minimal level of activity is achieved. Further evidence that the amount of protein made is important as the amount of catalytic activity acquired comes from the realisation that intracellular enzyme concentrations and intracellular substrate concentrations are of comparable magnitude. Thus the synthesis of a massive amount of a new protein may have dramatic effects on the free metabolite pool as a consequence of the ability of that protein to bind metabolites as well as a consequence of its catalytic abilities. The free oxaloacetate pool in a mitochondrion (i.e. the oxaloacetate found after denaturation of the mitochondrial protein with perchloric acid) is estimated to be about 5 μN whereas the concentration of oxaloacetate binding sites in a mitochondrion is at least 400 μN. The true concentration of 'free' oxaloacetate is thus much less than 5 μN and the synthesis, by a differentiating cell, of a mitochondrial protein which added to the concentration of the oxaloacetate binding sites might have effects, perhaps quite unconnected with the apparent enzymic activity of that protein. We are familiar with the idea of proteins acting as pH buffers and it is clear that they can, and probably do, act as buffers for substances other than and in

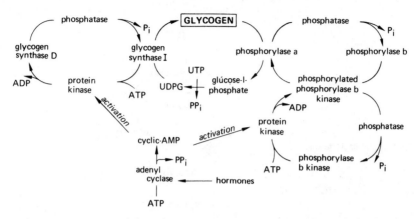

Fig. 4.17 Control of the level of glycogen in mammalian liver cells. Phosphorylase b and glycogen synthase D are not enzymically inactive but they differ in regulatory behaviour. Note that the controls are such that when glycogen synthase is in the I-form, phosphorylase is in the b form. Such a system of control, in which the modifying enzymes act catalytically on one another and on phosphorylase and glycogen synthase is called a 'cascade' since it acts to amplify the effects of small changes in hormone concentration.

addition to, the H⁺ ion. Until much more is known of the factors which regulate metabolic fluxes in cells, it is clearly difficult to discuss the relationship between the altered pattern of macromolecular syntheses seen during differentiation, and the altered metabolic capacities of the differentiated cell. From the discussion so far it is clearly naive, however, to assume that the relationship is necessarily simple or straight forward. Such little work that has been done on this topic suggests, in fact, that it is very complex (see p. 27).

The amount of glycogen in a mammalian liver, for example, is controlled by the activity of the glycogen synthetase enzyme (which catalyses the synthesis of glycogen) and phosphorylase (which catalyses the degradation of glycogen to glucose-1-phosphate). Both these enzymes exist in two forms which differ in their enzymic activity, their regulatory behaviour and the extent to which they are phosphorylated. The enzyme which catalyses the

phosphorylation of phosphorylase (Fig. 4.17) can itself exist in two forms which differ in their degree of phosphorylation and enzymic activity. The ubiquitous regulator molecule cyclic-AMP is involved at several stages in the overall scheme which seems extraordinarily and unnecessarily elaborate. The relationship between the activity of the genes regulating the amounts of these proteins synthesised by a liver cell during its differentiation and the need of the liver cell to regulate its glycogen content is also obscure. In fact, although the descriptive anatomy of cell differentiation is making great strides at the molecular level, the dynamic aspects of the process and its biochemical logic remain largely unexplored. Cyclic-AMP seems to be involved in the phosphorylation and thus regulation of a number of proteins from histones (p. 41) to phosphorylase, and a number of hormones, are known to stimulate the synthesis of cyclic-AMP but this is really little more than the hint of a clue as to how things might really 'work'.

59

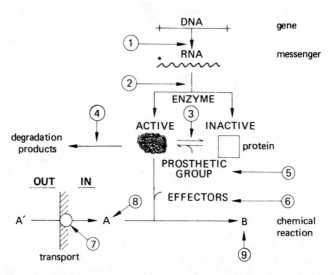

Fig. 4.18 Control points possible for regulation of a metabolic conversion of compound A to B during cell differentiation. 1 = transcription, 2 = translation, 3 = protein modification, 4 = protein degradation, 5 = alteration in concentration of prosthetic group, 6 = alteration in concentration of effector metabolites, 7 = transport phenomena, 8 and 9 = alteration in substrate or product concentrations.

Summary

During cell differentiation the rate at which a cell metabolite 'A' is converted to metabolite 'B' alters. As a consequence of the summation of such alterations, the structure and function of the cell changes and cell differentiation is the study of these changes. In Fig. 4.18 the levels at which the rate of conversion of 'A' to 'B' might be controlled, are indicated. These nine points are by no means exhaustive and the magnitude of the task facing developmental biologists can be appreciated when it is realised that the rate limiting step might change from one time to another or, at the same time, be different in cells in different positions in a cell mass. No doubt simplifying generalisations will appear and it will not be necessary to solve the problem presented in Fig. 4.18 for all A's and B's in all cells and for all times of development, but it is clear that the spectacular developments in our appreciation of what is involved in cell differentiation have removed little of the awe which inspired Aristotle when he wrote of this topic.

References

[1] Barth, L. J. (1964), *Development: Selected topics*, Addison Wesley, London.
[2] Paigen, K. (1971), In *Enzyme Synthesis and Degradation in Mammalian Systems*, Karger, Basel, 1–46.
[3] Callan, H. G. (1967), *J. Cell Sci.*, **2**, 1–7.
[4] Thomas, C. A. (1970), In *The Neurosciences: Second Study Program*, Rockefeller University Press, New York, 973–998.
[5] Ris, H. and Kubai, D. F. (1970), *Adv. in Genetics*, **4**, 263–294.
[6] Beerman, W. (1961), *Chromosoma*, **12**, 1–25.
[7] Grossbach, U. (1968), *Ann. Zool. Fennici.*, **5**, 37.

[8] Huang, R. C. C. and Kleiman, L. (1971), *Symp. Soc. Exp. Biol.*, **25**, 93–115.

[9] Paul, J. and Gilmour, R. S. (1968), *J. Mol. Biol.*, **34**, 305–316.

[10] Dixon, G. H. and Sung, M.T. (1970), *Proc. Nat. Acad. Sci.* (US), **67**, 1616–1623.

[11] Langan, T. A. (1968), *Science*, 162, 579–580.

[11a] Britten, R. J. and Davidson, E. H. (1969), *Science*, **165**, 349–357.

[12] Gall, J. and Pardue, M. L. (1969), *Proc. Nat. Acad. Sci.* (US), **63**, 378–383.

[13] Brown, D. D. and Dawid, I. B. (1968), *Science*, **160**, 272–280.

[14] Miller, O. L. and Beatty, B. R. (1969), *Science*, **164**, 955–957.

[15] Loening, U.E. (1970), *Symp. Soc. gen. Microbiol.*, **20**, 77–106.

[16] Pemberton, R. E., Housman, D., Lodish, H. F. and Baglioni, C. (1972), *Nature,* **235**, 99–102.

[17] Heywood, S. M. and Rich, A. (1968), *Proc. Nat. Acad. Sci.* (US), **59**, 590–597.

[18] Kedes, L. H. and Gross, P. (1969), *Nature*, **223**, 1335–1339.

[19] Kedes, L. H. and Birnsteil, M. L. (1971), *Nature,* **230**, 165–169.

[20] Bishop, J. O., Pemberton, R. and Baglioni, C. (1972), *Nature*, **235**, 231–234.

[21] Harris, H. (1969), *Cell Fusion*, Oxford University Press, Oxford.

[22] Felicetti, L., Gambino, R., Metafore, S. and Monroy, A. (1971), *Symp. Soc. Exp. Biol.*, **25**, 183–186.

[23] Heywood, S. M. (1970), *Nature*, **225**, 696–698.

[24] Lim, L. and Canellakis, E. G. (1970), *Nature*, **227**, 710–712.

[25] Williamson, A. (1969), In *Essays in Biochemistry*, **5**, 139–175.

[26] Schimke, R. T. (1969), In *Current Topics in Cellular Regulation,* **1**, 77–124.

[27] Markert, C. L. and Ursprung, H. (1971), *Developmental Genetics*, Prentice-Hall Inc., London.

[28] Wuntch, T., Chen, R. F. and Vessell, E. S. (1970), *Science*, 167, 63–65.

[29] Srere, P. A. (1967), *Science*, **158**, 936–937 and erratum on p. 1556.

[30] Brew, K. (1970), In *Essays in Biochemistry*, **6**, 93–118.

[31] Ashworth, J. M. (1971), *Symp. Soc. Exp. Biol.,* **25**, 27–50.

[32] Hess, B., Boiteux, A. and Kruger, J. (1969), In *Advances in Enzyme Regulation,* **7**, 149–167.

Suggestions for further reading

Introductory Books.

Newth, D. R. (1970). Animal Growth and Development. Studies in Biology no. 24. Edward Arnold Ltd.

Barth, L. J. (1964). Development: Selected Topics. Addison-Wesley Publishing Co., Ltd.

These two books are short introductions to the whole field of embryology and are especially recommended to those who know little of the subject.

Ebert, J. D. and Sussex, I. M. (1970). Interacting Systems in Development. 2nd. edition. Holt, Rinehart and Winston Inc.

Markert, C. L. and Ursprung, H. (1971). Developmental Genetics. Prentice-Hall Inc.

These two books have a molecular biology and biochemical emphasis, that by Ebert and Sussex also deals with plant development and that by Markert and Ursprung is particularily recommended for its treatment of isoenzymes.

Advanced Texts.

Balinsky, B. I. (1970). An Introduction to Embryology. W. B. Saunders Co.

Bodemer, C. W. (1968). Modern Embryology. Holt, Rinehart and Winston Inc.

There are few books on the modern view of the specifically biochemical aspects of cell differentiation. The following two books are useful summaries of work up to the time that they were published:

Deuchar, E. M. (1965). Biochemical Aspects of Amphibian Development. Methuen's Monographs on Biological Subjects. Methuen and Co., Ltd.

Brachet, J. (1960), The Biochemistry of Development. Pergamon Press.

Other books.

Two excellent collections of reprints of original papers have been published.

Bell, E. (1965). Molecular and Cellular Aspects of Development. Harper and Row.

Loomis, W. F. (1970). Papers on Regulation of Gene Activity during Development. Harper and Row.

A number of Learned Societies have recently held Symposia which deal with cell differentiation and Development. The proceedings of these have been published and no doubt more will appear shortly as interest in the subject continues to grow.

Smith, J. E. and Ashworth, J. M. (1973). Editors of Microbial Differentiation. 23rd. Symposium of the Society for General Microbiology. Cambridge University Press.

Davies, D. D. and Balls, M. (1971). Editors of Control Mechanisms of Growth and Differentiation. 25th. Symposium of the Society for Experimental Biology. Cambridge University Press.

Index